Interfaith Marriage

Interfaith Marriage

Working for World Peace at the Most Intimate Level

Edited by Bonni-Belle Pickard

*with Elizabeth Harris, Jonathan Romain,
David Grant, and Wendi Momen*

WIPF & STOCK · Eugene, Oregon

Wipf & Stock
An Imprint of Wipf and Stock Publishers
199 W. 8th Ave., Suite 3
Eugene, OR 97401

www.wipfandstock.com

PAPERBACK ISBN: 978-1-6667-3610-6
HARDCOVER ISBN: 978-1-6667-9396-3
EBOOK ISBN: 978-1-6667-9397-0

APRIL 18, 2022 10:38 AM

Permission kindly received from Naomi Schafer Riley for use of questions from her own interfaith marriage survey.

Dedicated to my parents, Bill and Annabelle Fisackerly,
with gratitude for all they taught me
about the realities of marriage and faith;

to my children—Lauren, Amanda, Raleigh, Benjamin, Tanya, Lara—
and their spouses,

with gratitude for all they taught me about the realities
of interfaith marriage;

and to my husband, Alfred,
with gratitude for his love, perseverance, and companionship.

Contents

List of Contributors

Bonni-Belle Pickard, Superintendent Minister with the Methodist Church in Britain. Previously Head of Music at Kodaikanal International School, S India. Her publications include *Extra Special Chocolate: Loving and Learning through International Adoption* and chapters in *Envisioning a New Heaven and a New Earth.*

Elizabeth J. Harris, Honorary Senior Research Fellow, The Edward Cadbury Centre for the Public Understanding of Religion, University of Birmingham (UK); former President, European Network of Buddhist-Christian Studies; and President of the UK Association for Buddhist Studies. Before retirement, she was an Associate Professor in Religious Studies at Liverpool Hope University. Between 1996 and 2007, she served as the Interfaith Relations Officer for the Methodist Church in Britain.

Jonathan Romain, rabbi of Maidenhead Synagogue, England, recently appointed as an Adviser to the Religion Media Centre, and often heard on the BBC. He received the MBE for work with mixed-faith couples in Britain, a theme covered in his book, *Till Faith Us Do Part.*

David Grant, retired social worker and management consultant, member of the Bahá'í community for over fifty years, and a founding member of the Maidstone Inter-Faith Network.

Wendi Momen, publisher and educator; trustee and director of the National Spiritual Assembly of the Bahá'ís of the United Kingdom for over thirty years; treasurer of Bedford Council of Faiths. She is the author of thirteen books on the Bahá'í faith.

Preface

2021 IS COMING TO AN END as I return to this manuscript on interfaith marriage, which I've been working on for many years. My interest in the subject first arose out of the experiences of family and friends involved with interfaith relationships, some of which developed into marriages. Their commitment to communicating faithfully, lovingly, and intimately across cultural boundaries fascinated me. I also recognized the challenges these relationships posed for the couples, their families, and their faith communities, all of whom struggled in some way to understand and accept new ways of relating. I wanted to learn more about how to make these relationships flourish for all involved.

As I set out to explore what led to successful interfaith marriages, I recognized that while *interfaith* marriages were often *intercultural* marriages, and while some would classify the *interfaith* as a subset of *intercultural*, there were significant differences as well. My explorations rapidly became a project which emphasized for me the importance of the *faith* dimension of marriage.

I also became more aware that interfaith marriages, like all marriages, involve a good deal of conflict resolution techniques: when two or more different perspectives are at work, inevitably conflict arises. How we work through those conflicts establishes whether we are able to proceed peaceably and with respect for each other. Ultimately, our ability to grow is linked to our ability to resolve and accommodate conflict. Marriage remains the most intimate and prolonged human endeavor in conflict resolution. When we add in disparate understandings from the interfaith or intercultural, there is enormous potential for growth as well as for conflict.

As 2021 draws to a close, the global community is cautiously trying to venture out from the social restrictions of a prolonged pandemic. On the one hand, the numbers of those wanting to get married have soared even while many of those already married have faced many strains on their marriage and family life due to periods of social confinement. Apart from the stress of little relief from being with each other day after day, opportunities for informal chats with family and friends—or with professional counsellors—have been reduced or consigned to virtual conversations. Virtual chats were initially a welcome chance to interact with others safely during the pandemic, but they had their limits. Many soon learned they could tilt the camera to just show what they wanted to be seen, and so put on a different mask that could prevent real understanding or communication. Gatherings of faith communities likewise took on a different dimension as access to the informal aspect of such comings-together were reduced. Still my own research and virtual seminars have continued and been well-received with folks near and far. I've realized again the importance of providing resources to help people work through interfaith and marital matters on their own.

As we're approaching the end of the lockdowns, weddings are all around. This past summer, the Methodist Church in Britain formally adopted far-reaching exploration of marriage and relationships that has, among other things, set the stage for Methodist churches to allow same-sex marriages on their premises. This move, while still opposed by many in Christian churches at large, comes after many decades of theological reflection—and a few years after the UK government changed its laws on the same. The Methodist report also has formally begun a radical rethinking of cohabitation and what faithful, committed, loving relationships look like in the twenty-first century. Some are accusing the Methodist Church in Britain of selling out to social pressure. Others recognize that church and society have always pushed each other to consider new perspectives. This is another form of essential dialogue that helps us each to be our best. An important part of the Methodist conversations at present is an affirmation that marriage is the ideal relationship for developing "self-giving love, commitment, fidelity, loyalty, honesty, mutual respect, equality, and the desire for the mutual flourishing of the people involved."[1] That definition resounds with the understanding of marriage of my own studies.

---

1. Trustees for Methodist Church Purposes, "Marriage and Relationships," 2:814.

Acknowledgments

My grateful thanks to:

Wesley Theological Seminary's Cambridge B DMin track, especially Sathianathan Clarke, who steered my project through its research stages; my classmates: Lisa Arledge, Herbert Brisbon, Grainger Browning, Michelle Grove, Kong Ching Hii, Richard Hoffman, Don Kuntz, Beth Ludlum, Malcolm Stranathan, Cynthia Moore-Koikoi, Jean Claude Masuka Maleka, and Nick Works; and Bruce Birch and Carole Irwin, who kept believing in us.

Mentors and teachers from Candler School of Theology, who taught me how to do theology: Mary Elizabeth Moore, Joy McDougall, Ten Runyon, Thomas Thangaraj, and Desmond Tutu.

Colleagues at Kodaikanal International School who stretched my understanding of faith, especially Martha and John Easter, Mark Garrison, Raja Krishnamoorthy, Priscilla Mohl, Rocky and Jerry Nichol, Ian Oliver, Cass Shaw, and Paul Wiebe. Special thanks to current Principal Corey Stixrud for stimulating my thinking on how the school's emphasis on faith development affected its students' ability to interact across faith boundaries into their later life.

KIS alumni who took the time and interest to respond to my survey.

The brave couples and individuals who allowed me to interview and/or trial my Intervention Protocol on them.

Arasu Israel and Beulah "Billy" Kolhatkar, who assisted my research at American College, Madurai, S. India, as well as the students and staff who eagerly answered my questions about their engagements with interfaith marriage.

The North Kent Methodist Circuit and colleagues for support and grant funding for my doctoral program; the South East Methodist District and the Methodist Church in Britain for further grant funding.

Acknowledgments

Rosalind Birtwistle, Heather-Jane Ozanne, and Jill Marsh for sharing experiences and interfaith marriage contacts.

Maidstone Interfaith Network for enthusiastic support.

Mary Rees, Amy Evans, and Jim Bryant for careful proofreading efforts—along with those of my recently deceased mother, Annabelle Fisackerly, whose last coherent words to me were: "How's your book coming along?"

Abbreviations of Scriptures

Hebrew Bible/Old Testament

Gen = Genesis

Song = Song of Solomon (Song of Songs)

Deut = Deuteronomy

Exod = Exodus

Num = Numbers

New Testament

Matt = Matthew

1 Cor = First Corinthians

Eph = Ephesians

Gal = Galatians

Qur'an

Q = Qur'an

Hindu Scriptures

Gita = Bhagavad Gita

R = Ramayana

PART ONE

*Exploring Issues and Tools
for Supporting Interfaith Marriage*

Introduction

I WAS NEARLY SEVEN when I fell in love with my Jewish classmate, Kenneth. Though we hardly ever spoke, he would write me love notes on tiny scraps of paper which I kept stashed in the corner of my desk. After his delightful explanation of Hanukkah during Show-and-Tell—complete with dreidel and menorah—I spent many hours trying to decide if the daughter of a Methodist minister could marry a Jew. As it happened, our puppy love evaporated the next year when we were put in different classes, but I was set with a lifelong interest in different faith backgrounds.

My interest in other faiths was not an indication that I was dissatisfied with my own; I was simply intrigued to learn how others approached theirs. Looking back, Kenneth was probably the first person I had met who was not Methodist or Baptist or Catholic. Being part of a Methodist minister's family meant my four siblings and I were usually at some kind of church activities if we were not at school or music lessons. My growing-up years were spent in Florida, and Methodist ministers there moved frequently, so we learned a good bit about adjusting to new experiences, even as our church experiences remained fairly constant from place to place. My father's brand of Methodism was liberal; his intention to live out his theology in practical forms had a deep influence on me, which was especially important as my growing-up years in the Deep South also coincided with the Civil Rights movement and desegregation of the schools, the Women's Liberation movement, and the advent of the Pill.

The man I eventually married was also Methodist; we met at Florida Southern College, a Methodist institution from which most of my family had graduated and would subsequently graduate. Alfred and I were each one of five children and were both music majors, so we shared many interests and childhood family experiences. There was, however, one major difference: while I had grown up in Florida, my husband had been born

3

and raised in India to missionary parents. While our faith backgrounds were similar, there were many times when the cultural differences of our childhood presented themselves unannounced. My earliest memory of him was noticing that he wore flip-flops to school (he called them by the Indian term, rubber chappals); even though I'd grown up in Florida, nobody else I knew wore flip-flops to school! With several cultural differences to negotiate, our similar faith background seemed like something to hold on to.

Soon after our wedding in Florida, we moved to South India to teach music at the boarding school Alfred had attended for most of his childhood education. We stayed at Kodaikanal International School for the next twenty years, living and working with a wide variety of cultures and religious backgrounds. During those two decades we collected and raised our six children: three from my womb, and three from my heart (one adopted Tamil Indian and two fostered Parsi Indians).

By the time our own children became young adults, they seemed unconcerned with the social uncertainties about interfaith marriage that had colored my childhood. They simply married their soul mates: life partners from Islam, Atheism, Buddhism, Hinduism, Catholicism and other Protestant traditions (no Methodists!). Their spouses' families have come from the USA, England, Libya, India, Switzerland, and China. In the meantime, our family moved from India to the USA and then to the UK; our children and grandchildren currently live on three continents. Their families are intercultural and interfaith. Our children have taught me about the wider canvas on which God paints Godself in our lives.

Observing our children's marriages and subsequent family lives pushed me to dig deeper into understanding how culture and faith are often intricately woven together. As an avid knitter, I know that knitting means making a new cloth out of long pieces of preexisting string. When two or more different strands are used, new shapes and patterns emerge—as well as the occasional seemingly insurmountable knots. A certain perseverance is required for keeping track of the various strands and how they best work together—and how to unpick the knots.

One of the knots that has seemed most difficult for interfaith couples is the faith dimension. When people would hear that I was researching interfaith marriage, inevitably they assumed I focused on the wedding part of the marriage. There are indeed several books and articles dedicated to giving tips about how to put together a ceremony that accommodates diverse faith traditions. I looked at several of them when my children (and others) asked me, as a minister in the British Methodist Church, to contribute to their wedding ceremonies. But even though putting together a coherent wedding ceremony was an interesting venture, I knew that while some weddings might last less than an hour (or several days in the case of a Hindu wedding), a marriage is usually meant to last a lifetime. Indeed, it probably takes a lifetime to get a marriage right. The long haul is required for deeper faith realities to emerge through the day-to-day living out of relationships: the marriages.

In much young adult culture today around the world there has been a general dismissal of religion even as there remains a searching for spirituality and a dim awareness of the importance of individual and communal faith development. For many, the growing awareness of other religions has been a source of confusion, if not outright conflict. Trying to reconcile competing religious beliefs and practices has been considered as too difficult, especially in an interfaith relationship. It has been easier to regard oneself and one's interfaith marriage as not religious.

My life experience tells me the easy option is not the best: each individual and each couple has the responsibility and the privilege to grow into spiritually mature persons. Those who are brave enough to take on an *interfaith marriage* are signaling such a willingness to think again. In the first place, they show a willingness to consider matrimony when cohabitation is rapidly becoming the worldwide norm, and they are pushing the traditional boundaries of wedlock into a supportive foundation for mutual growth and familial stability. Secondly, for those who choose a marriage partner from another faith tradition, the issues of religion and spirituality (i.e., faith) can take on new dimensions. Still, as society at large sifts through the challenges of what has been and what might be, there are few ready answers for what will actually work now.

My research efforts over the past few years have been to glean through faith traditions of marriage to see what can be recovered, rescued, or salvaged for use in our present circumstances, especially for those attempting interfaith marriage in an age that generally favors equality and respect. As one who tends toward a liberal worldview, I am acutely aware of the noisy rise of fascism, nationalism, sexism, and racism in the public arena, but I also regard these as aberrations in the overall arch toward God's kingdom of justice and peace for all.

As a person of faith, I am interested in how marriage and faith intersect in the development of personal spiritual maturity. I continue to learn from listening to those with little regard for either marriage or faith, but too often that disregard seems to arise either from a personal encounter with the worst of these institutions or from a distorted view of the aims of the institutions. I also recognize there are infinite shades of difference in belief and practice in all faith traditions, and that caricatures of these abound, especially about matters of faith that are different from one's own. Particularly when writing about other faith traditions, I have sought to find the best each has to offer, recognizing that there are skeletons in all our closets.

While I hope that what I have to offer will be of benefit to many, I have embarked on this research from and for the perspective of Methodist Christians. There is much for us to learn as well about ourselves, our beliefs and practices, as well as the "other." As a Methodist minister, I am aware that a new skillset is required, not just for interfaith couples and their families, but for those of us who are willing to accompany them on their journeys.

A final introductory note: while the experiences of my children and their spouses gave impetus to much of my study, this book is not all about them and their experiences. The personal stories I have included as illustrations are those for which I have gained permission, either from my children or those who offered to share with me during the course of my research. While sharing our stories is important, preserving the dignity of trust and a respect for each other's privacy is also paramount to maintaining good relationships. Their stories are their own. My children did not ask me to be their mother, nor have they asked me to write a book about them. I trust my readers will find within these pages impetus for exploring their own stories and sharing them as they feel comfortable with those who might need to hear in order to better understand.

CHAPTER 1

Rethinking and Reshaping Marriage
as an Institution

"MY HEART SAYS 'YES.' Parents say 'no.'"[1] So tweeted a lovelorn young woman not so long ago. Her plight reflects a twenty-first-century phenomenon: Is my life my own, or does it belong to the wider society? Is the choice of my life's partner to be dictated by my own desires, or the needs of my community? The rapidly increasing number of interfaith marriages across the world has further intensified the question in recent years, but in reality, her situation reflects larger changes in perceptions of marriage that have been emerging across the globe for quite a while.

Several decades ago, my mother was not happy with my decision to walk down the aisle wearing a hat instead of a veil. It was part of my mid-1970s statement about entering my marriage commitment as a free and equal partner, rather than being hidden behind a mask of gauze. In retrospect, the stylish floppy hat I chose (with daisies around the crown) covered a good part of my face in several of the photos anyway. In Momma's day—the mid-1950s—having a traditional wedding and all the formal appearances was very important, even though I found out later she'd refused to say the traditional vows, instead reciting the famous lines from Ruth in the Bible, "Whither thou goest, I will go" (Ruth 1:16b KJV), to her Methodist preacher husband. Our own children and nieces and nephews have married in churches (the brides mostly veiled), in a front garden, on the beach, at a country club, and in a register office. Whereas my parents paid for a

1. Arushi Kapoor@curlmoohi, 3 Aug 2016, http://viralsection.com/hilarious-tweets-joys-pains-growing-desi-will-crack/ (link no longer active).

significant part of our fairly simple wedding (which meant Momma felt her objection to my apparel was justified), by the time the last of our offspring tied the knot, he and his fiancée made far more money than we did, so they paid for virtually all of the elaborate occasion. Wedding customs have changed in our own lifetimes.

Marriage as an institution has changed as well. Some changes which seem to have happened virtually overnight have been brewing for decades, if not centuries. From being an institution to secure family lines and property and economic/political stability to becoming a relationship based on love, the concept of marriage itself has changed along with altered expectations and assumptions about matrimony. Many have wondered whether marriage is an outmoded institution, an unnecessary form of bondage, an outdated way of imposing regulations on one's body, mind, and soul. While many traditional marriage customs seem archaic in the twenty-first century, there is value in going back to think again. What were the original purposes and aims of marriage? What benefits have arisen from the institution? Are there ways to refit it for contemporary use while recognizing or alleviating the intended and unintended consequences?

Roots

The original concept of marriage grew out of a need to regulate sexual activity and provide familial/tribal stability and security in human society. Like all species, humans need to reproduce to survive. Biologically the human male is relatively unencumbered with responsibilities for his sexual activity, but the extended period of pregnancy and the care needed during the comparatively slow early development of human offspring means that *homo sapiens* women and children are physically vulnerable for a longer time than nearly any other species. A system of familial care to protect this vulnerability was crucial to the survival of the developing human species. Accommodating and caring for this vulnerability led to an adoption of prescribed complementary roles for men and women: she would produce and nurture offspring; he would protect and provide. These patterns for stable family units which supported women and children in their vulnerability became established as the foundations of patriarchal society.

Regulated sexual activity enhanced social stability by providing healthy and consistent outlets for sexual activity within marriage and by creating cohesive family groups. Issues of property, inheritance, and family line came to be defined through marriage relationships. Linking families with long-term monogamous pairing eventually becoming the norm for most stable societies.[2] Stephanie Coontz, in her book, *Marriage, a History,* notes that families linking together through marriage raised the possibility of turning "strangers into relatives and enemies into allies."[3] This was especially important to the political power-wielding of the wealthy, who could strategically forge peace treaties through marriages of their offspring.[4] For the poorer segments of society, marriage fostered the economics of family and village survival. As Coontz notes: "Few individuals of modest means had either the inclination or the opportunity to seek a soul mate. What they really needed was a work partner."[5]

And yet, long-term coupling—even if it had originated in a system of regulation for sexual relations and the rearing of offspring, for interfamilial bonding and political and economic strengthening—also provided opportunities for those involved to develop personal maturity. As the individual took increased responsibility for others as well as him/herself, s/he learned about empathy, trust, setting of boundaries, negotiation, and even forgiveness. Marriage had the potential to provide partners with companionship and mutual protection, even if their unions were established primarily as economic or political necessities.

The most ancient religious understandings of procreation recognized something of the divine in sexual pairings. Even as most religions moved beyond associating human sexuality with divine fertility cults, a recognition of the sacredness in human sexuality remained, particularly in the sense of creativity, in physical and spiritual union, and perhaps even in love. In the fullest expression of a marital relationship, spiritual maturity also was nurtured; nearly all religions would point to marriage as an opportunity to further develop an understanding of divine love and faithfulness.

Procreation, the ordering of society in stable family units, personal maturity, and spiritual development thus took their places as fundamental purposes of marriage, though cultures and eras varied in how they ranked

2. In their paper on "Evolutionary History of Hunter-Gatherer Marriage Practices," Walker et al. explore how tribal security was a crucial factor in the development of marriage, with parents/tribes responsible for choosing their descendants' sex partners. They also point out that humans are virtually the only primates to choose sex partners from other "tribes."

3. Coontz, *Marriage, a History,* 44.

4. Coontz, *Marriage, a History,* 6.

5. Coontz, *Marriage, a History,* 68.

these values. Nearly all traditions regarded marriage as a social construct between families around which religious rites developed. Families came together to bless marital unions and communally ask divine blessing on the couple and their eventual offspring. The patriarchal assumptions of the need for regulating sexual activity and assigning male and female roles for child-raising and household management in turn became part of communal religious understandings.

Contemporary Challenges

The twentieth century saw several pivotal societal changes which dramatically affected the institution of marriage. The arrival in the 1960s of The Pill as a safe, reliable, and readily available form of birth control for women unleashed a sexual revolution which radically challenged the traditional institution of marriage as a necessary regulator of sexual activity.[6] Parallel to the invention and availability of birth control for women was a growing concern that the human population was exploding at unsustainable rates. If procreation was no longer mandated or desirable, was there any purpose for marriage?

As a woman gained control of her own reproductive system, she also realized she had the potential to control how and when she would participate in employment, education, and leisure outside the family home. Many couples took stock of their own marriages; if they had only stayed together for sexual activity or financial stability, those needs could be satisfied in other ways. Meanwhile, the Women's Liberation movement of the mid-to-late twentieth century fostered an understanding of gender equality that, while not yet completely fulfilled, permeated most of Western and indeed global society and altered marital assumptions about gender roles, particularly those enshrined in patriarchy.

The dismantling of patriarchal assumptions of marriage also affected men. Gradually, Western states, with their social welfare systems, had taken upon themselves some of the male patriarchal roles, especially assuming some financial responsibility for women and children when the husband/father figure was not able to do so (usually because of war or a need to travel). That principle was very much in effect when the sexual revolution of the 1960s and 1970s also gave men more sexual freedom. With fewer absolute responsibilities and more sexual freedom, the traditional marriage

6. Gibbs, "Pill at 50."

roles for males were questioned. In her work on emerging adults, Sharon Daloz Parks explores the question: As women expanded their roles in society, what did society require of men? "Young men are discovering that their traditional roles—procreate, provide, and protect—are being significantly recast in new gender role assumptions, an overpopulated planet, a globalized economy (in which increasingly "brain" trumps "brawn"), and the changing conditions of warfare."[7]

As couples began to explore gender equity in their lives together, the uncertainty of the new order often made difficult demands on day-to-day relationships. The state may have taken on responsibility, particularly financial, for times of domestic vulnerability, but couples began to realize that the state could not provide the sense of belonging, companionship, and mutual giving that marriage afforded. The vulnerability question, which once related primarily to protecting *women* in pregnancy and childbirth, was now considered more often in terms of providing stability for *children*; indeed, most young couples who cohabit for extended periods decide to marry when children are expected or have arrived.

Others have pointed out that what is termed "cohabitation" today would have been recognized as "marriage" in other times and places. In the contemporary context, perhaps a key distinguisher is the intent of the couple to make a public (and legal) statement about the ongoing and covenantal status of their relationship. Many would argue that such a statement is no longer needed, especially when many of the practical needs of the couple and their children are cared for by the state.[8]

While it is argued that these personal and practical relationship needs can be met in long-term cohabitation arrangements, often extended familial ties are weak at best when couples decide only to live together. In many cases, a couple which opts out of marriage also implicitly opts out of family blessing,[9] so that lack of communal support becomes even more acute.

In a parallel development, interfaith marriage researcher Erika Seamon has argued that, by the end of the twentieth century in America, the concept of marriage as a religious or familial covenant had been supplanted

---

7. Parks, *Big Questions, Worthy Dreams*, 7.

8. Paradoxically, many contemporary Western legal systems meant to support vulnerable persons (particularly unwed mothers and their children) in reality promote cohabitation rather than marriage.

9. Jo McGowan, "Marriage versus Living Together," 85.

by an understanding of marriage as a "love-based institution."[10] Coontz traces this movement back further to developments in the eighteenth century.[11] My own research and that of others indicates that this trend is not peculiar to the USA but has become firmly entrenched in European society and gained popularity around the world. British author Jonathan Romain speaks of the "search for individual happiness"[12] as the major impetus for marriages in the UK, claiming that marriage is:

> . . . no longer [merely] the union of two families, . . . [nor] the prerogative of family heads, with the actual bride and groom being incidental players. Instead it is a personal matter for the couple concerned, with the family being the bystander. Compatibility is not only judged by the two partners but is seen as being dependent on their feelings for each other. Love is the determining factor.[13]

Coontz also points out that the development of the love-based marriage standard and the accompanying criteria of personal satisfaction has led both to the sexualization of the contemporary age and an instability of marriage as an institution. Coontz claims: "The very features that promised to make marriage such a unique and treasured relationship opened the way for it to become an optional and fragile one."[14] She notes that, as the love-based model predominated: "People began marrying later. Divorce rates soared. Premarital sex became the norm."[15]

The relaxation of sexual regulation has in turn fostered an intimacy crisis in contemporary society. The widespread availability of multiple sexual partners means sexual activity is often disconnected from the development of long-term relationships. The freedom to change partners at will (albeit usually in a pattern of serial monogamy) disrupts social stability and can prevent the development of personal maturity traits that come through intentional long-term pairings, traits such as fidelity and the capacity of forgiveness for shortcomings. A new type of vulnerability is emerging especially in men: suicide is presently the leading cause of death amongst

10. Seamon, *interfaith marriage in America*, 71.

11. Coontz, *Marriage, a History*, 5.

12. Romain, *Till Faith Us Do Part*, 17.

13. Romain, *Till Faith Us Do Part*, 51.

14. Coontz, *Marriage, a History*, 5.

15. Coontz, *Marriage, a History*, 247.

young males in the UK, with some experts citing the breakdown of marital relations as a major factor.[16]

By the end of the twentieth century, the parents of emerging adults were primarily Baby Boomers who recognized that many of the changes in marital assumptions had emerged from the sexual experimentation of their own generation. They were (and are) reluctant to interfere with their adult children's choices,[17] and, in an unstable global economic climate, are often more eager to see their children settled in their careers before getting married.[18] Meanwhile, incompatibility has become the major reason for divorce, hinting that perhaps personal development has become the most sought-after aspect of marriage. Meanwhile, the significant increase in legal (and social) acceptance of same-sex marriages indicates that procreation has indeed been demoted as the main purpose of sexual relations.

All these factors point to marriage as an institution in a state of flux. While many of the original purposes of marriage have been severely questioned, perhaps it is its "faith, hope, and love" aspects—those virtues celebrated in 1 Corinthians 13:13, often quoted at Christian weddings—which remain attractive as constructive ways to mature personally, socially, and spiritually. The phenomenon of interfaith marriages adds still another layer of relationships to explore: Is it possible or desirable to reconcile diverse cultural understandings of marriage? For now, we turn our attention to another set of institutions which have struggled in recent times: that of religion and faith communities.

16. Parker, "What Can We Do?"
17. Riley, *'Til Faith Do Us Part*, 42.
18. Riley, *'Til Faith Do Us Part*, 53.

Chapter 2

Rethinking Religion as an Institution

ONE WARM EARLY SUMMER morning in 2020, I was standing in full, black-robed Methodist ministerial regalia at a North London cemetery gravesite, preparing for the funeral of the father of a dear friend. Even if the pandemic restrictions had not been in place, we probably would not have been commemorating L's funeral in a church, as he usually avoided churches. I knew L mostly through informal family gatherings with his son and daughter-in-law, a Christian and Jewish interfaith couple, and their three children. I had been present for the youngest grandchild's circumcision as well as conducting his subsequent baptism. That had happened some fifteen years before, but we had kept in touch when I had been moved on to a different circuit.[1] When the funeral request came from my friends, I was sad for their loss, somewhat surprised to still be included in their personal lives, but happy to oblige.

We had worked out the order of service via Zoom, and I was going through it in my mind when I heard a distinctive *clip-clop* in the distance and spied the formal hearse being drawn down the path by four splendid black horses. L was certainly going out in style! Soon we gathered ourselves around the open grave (appropriately socially-distanced), sharing prayers and hymns and readings and reminding each other of a life well lived. We all recited Psalm 23, I read a passage from John's Gospel, one of the grandsons read from the prophet Isaiah, and his sister and mother intoned a

---

1. British Methodist churches are organized into local federations known as "circuits," and British Methodist ministers traditionally move on to different circuits about every five years.

haunting a capella *Adon Olam* in Hebrew and English. When the scorching sun threatened to get the better of all of us, we had laid the coffin and L to rest in the ground and slowly walked back to our cars, singing, "I am a poor wayfaring stranger."

Chatting later in the afternoon, my friend told me his dad had specifically requested I do his funeral because he knew "it would be the way he wanted it to be." My friend also related the story of L's mother's funeral, shortly after the end of the Second World War, when times were still difficult, and L was a fourteen-year-old boy. Apparently, the vicar had made a very perfunctory job of the funeral, and L was distraught at the seeming insensitivity and impersonal nature of it all. Young L vowed at that point never to enter a church again. Hearing the story, I was amazed to recall that indeed L had come to a few of my services. "He knew you were different and would make it personal," came the reply.

Roots of Religion

"Making it personal" sums up the yearning for the personal connection—between ourselves and the divine, between ourselves and each other—that is at the heart of being human. It is the essence of the word *religio,* which comes from a word meaning "to link/bind together." When religion is done impersonally, we are repulsed, as was dear L and so many others. When religion becomes an institution instead of a relationship, it is rightfully questioned by society, and the time comes, as it has with marriage, to think again about its place in society. For faith communities, this rethinking often comes in cycles as we question why we do what we do, how we might purge our systems of unhelpful (or even abusive) practices, and how we can discover again new and better ways to make meaning of our lives.

The great spiritual awakenings of the past all followed times of deep frustration with, and turning away from, religious traditions that seemed stuffy, outmoded, or insufficient for the current age. Indeed, so many changes have occurred in our world over the past several decades that "thinking again" becomes an essential task. For some, times of uncertainty mean clinging to rituals and traditions regardless of whether they fit the current age. Others reject the whole system. Somewhere in the midst of that chaos we catch a glimpse again of purpose and meaning behind the traditions. Without becoming suffocated in nostalgia, we do well to metaphorically sift through what we've discarded to find the gems worth polishing again.

Seeking Meaning

Human consciousness sets our species apart from others. We are aware not just of ourselves and the environment around us, but somehow our minds also allow us to observe ourselves, to try to make sense of ourselves and our surroundings, and to try to connect with a greater force beyond ourselves. From the earliest nights spent gazing at the pricks of light shining through unfathomable darkness, we've tried to make sense of who we are and what is beyond us; the vastness of that dark beyond reminded us of our frailty and our vulnerability even as we were aware of our own capacities to do and be, and to change the world around us. The key was recognizing the balance between the powers beyond and within ourselves. Perhaps that search for balance was the beginning of religion.

Searching for the balance between self and all the Others—be they other people or creatures, the natural environment, or forces we began to speak of in guarded whispers—meant careful observation, trial and error, and response. We learned what worked and what did not work. We passed on the information about our successes and failures through story and song and dance and example. We shared our assembled wisdom to help ourselves and each other make sense of the Other, of what had happened in the past, what was happening to us now, and what might happen in the future if we continued with what we were doing. As we passed on our stories, we passed on our consciousness, our understanding of what was beyond ourselves. Especially in those lessons which seemed particularly wrapped in mystery, such as birth and death, and love and pain, and sacrifice and joy, we recognized something sacred, and we developed rituals to help us remember, commemorate, and celebrate.

Our rituals, in turn, helped forge bonds between ourselves. These bonds strengthened our communities, making us stronger against outside threats. Communal survival had more guarantees than individual survival, and the rituals reminded us we belonged to something larger than ourselves. Our shared beliefs relieved us of each having to reinvent the wheel, and yet, individual experiences could also inform the whole group. We told each other our stories, and we collectively sifted and weighed them. If they resonated with the group, they became part of the collective story. Those stories which supported the persons with the most power became public property; those stories which resonated with the less-powerful often went underground, nevertheless becoming more potent in the solidarity they fostered with less-powerful others.

In the process, religion created bonds of belonging and belief within the group as well as with that which is beyond. The binding allowed security, especially important for the earliest societies, when threats were all around. Strong bonds enabled communities to contend not just with the forces of nature—drought and floods, heat and cold, eating and being eaten—but at times with how to deal with each other. Though nearly all our religious traditions speak of an original man and woman, they soon speak of strife erupting between the two as they recognized their differences. We humans learned how to distinguish between our own tribes and protect ourselves from those we perceived as being dissimilar. As we set up our systems of religious belief, we also established our tribal gods, with our understanding of the universal often encumbered by our own particularities. When our separate tribes encountered each other again, it was often our differences that were most apparent. To protect ourselves, we learned to spot those differences well—and to fight against the other in self-preservation.

And yet nearly all our religious traditions also espoused the need for kindness in dealing with others. There is a nearly universal understanding that generosity and hospitality are most effective ways to ultimately ensure one's well-being, that one's own well-being is intricately connected with the well-being of the Other. Systems of power, with one over the other, only produced harmony when the power invested was used to ensure the well-being of the whole. When the power became corrupted to enforce the will of one at the expense of the whole, the notions of kindness and generosity that lead to peace were subverted.

As our human communities gradually expanded and diversified, from time to time we would come back in contact with those with whom we had been estranged. In some cases, the family tree had become so prolific and diverse that we no longer recognized each other as family. In our competition for the resources we felt we needed, we began to see the other as enemy, and our differences became more pronounced and took on a supposed additional imperative.

Those foundational truths of our common heritage still come back to remind us: we are all connected. If we destroy each other, we destroy ourselves. As I write this, our world is in the grips of a pandemic lockdown which, even while it has forced us all to think again about self-preservation, has also reminded us that we're all in this together. The identification of differences that have often become so engrained in our imaginations also point us toward our misuse of power against each other. Those who are most vulnerable also need the most protection.

Nearly all faith traditions have at least one creation story, an attempt to grasp why we came to be. Those stories necessarily highlight certain aspects that faith traditions value, such as order, goodness, continuity. The stories also reveal an understanding of *being created*: that a force exists which is greater than what has been created. Whether that force is called Yahweh or God or Allah or Ahura Mazda or Shakti or Mother Nature, something came before and is bigger than we are; especially in times of confusion we do well to explore original sources again for what we might learn. There we glimpse afresh that sense of the cosmic sacred that can inform our own little worlds. From there we can weigh again the *beliefs* we have received against the reality we have perceived.

Contemporary Challenges

In the millennia of human travel since our earliest days of staring at the nighttime sky, we have become increasingly less able to look beyond ourselves to see the stars. Years ago, I discovered in one of Madeleine L'Engle's books that the word *dis-aster* literally means "being separated from the stars." She's using the word "disaster" to refer in part to the light pollution of our cities, which means many of us can no longer see the stars at night, but she also writes in *A Stone for a Pillow*, "When we are separated from the stars, the sea, each other, we are in danger of being separated from God."[2]

Separated from God, separated from each other, separated from the natural environment . . . and finding ourselves alone and isolated. Ironically, perhaps the loneliness of our contemporary world has been fostered in part by the coming together physically of our diversity—what we could call globalization—but coming together without having retained the tools for *how* we are to be together.

We've remembered how we are to protect ourselves—and our religion—from dangerous outside influences, but we have forgotten that we are ultimately all made of the same stardust, all created by the same Creator, whether we envision that Creator as a careful molder of body-mind-spirit, or a mad flinger of cosmic dust who flung often enough that various bits of dust collided and formed us. The argument that religion is all about making God in our own image also reveals that our understanding of God is at least

2. L'Engle, *Stone for a Pillow*, 17.

in part formed by our understanding (or misunderstanding) of ourselves. Where we have got our understanding wrong is surely more our own fault than the Creator's.

When our religious traditions bump up against each other, it is easy enough to claim our own is better, wiser, truer, more complete, the only way. But the "my way is best/my way is the only way" tactic is also part of our own egotistic tendency for self-protection. It leads others to become defensive and has led many to discard religion entirely. Far wiser to listen deeply to the truths that others bring and thus cultivate a culture of shared vulnerability and therefore shared strength.

Still for some, all religion is to be rejected. Especially in contemporary European society, humanism has become a strident voice against what it sees as outmoded faith traditions, though Theo Hobson and others have posited that secular humanism grew out of Christian religious beliefs.[3] Others have decided that science is their religion, and that adherence to the scientific method precludes the necessity of faith. John Hedley Brooke, in *Science and Religion,* has convincingly demonstrated how the current understanding of science and the scientific method grew out of the religious quest for truth and understanding that developed what we know as scientific reason to support its principles. He notes that science, in turn, historically used religious belief to investigate its own truth searches. The present presumed adversarial relationship between science and religion helps neither side understand either itself or the Other. Many who remain within faith traditions are frustrated that much of what the outside world rejects as faith tenets, they, too, reject. As the Protestant Reformation coincided with the Counter-Reformation of the Roman Catholic Church, many faith traditions have continued the age-old pattern of reviewing and reconsidering belief patterns for their fit with contemporary challenges, even as some have resolutely clung to outmoded beliefs and practices.

Still, in today's world, many are declaring themselves atheists, agnostics, nonbelievers, or nones. The latter category has in fact seen the largest increase in adherents over recent decades; in the US, The Pew Research Center has seen a rise of nonbelievers from 17 percent in 2009 to 26 percent in 2019.[4] Sociologist Grace Davie observes in Europe how the trend

3. Hobson, *God Created Humanism.*

4. Pew Research Center, "In U.S., Decline," para. 1. My own survey of alumni of Kodaikanal International School in S. India indicates that the number of those claiming to be non-believers peaked in the 1980s with about 20 percent, and thereafter declined to about 8 percent in 2018.

toward shunning structured religion and traditional faith approaches has been going on for much longer even as the search for spirituality remains.[5]

We have spoken of religion in the context of community and communal harmony, but our contemporary context also emphasizes the importance of individualism, itself an outgrowth of the Protestant Reformation. The drive toward the individual rather than the group identity has grown, first in the Western world and then further afield. Along these lines, Diana Butler Bass, in *Christianity After Religion,* argues that much contemporary spiritual development in the Western world is being done on a personal level, outside of—or seemingly *in spite* of—established faith traditions, in this case, particularly, the church.[6] "I'm spiritual, but I'm not religious," has become a popular mantra, which Scotty McLennan, author of *Finding Your Religion: When the Faith You Grew Up with Has Lost Its Meaning,* interprets as "I have my own way that's not related to some group or organization or institution."[7]

The popularity of finding one's own spirituality comes at the cost of communal harmony, which, as we've seen, is an essential part of that original *religio* that, at its best, seeks to unite individuals into community. An emphasis on each individual seeking out personal spirituality leads to poverty for all, and limits the individual to his/her own resources. McLennan points out that today's secular world often dismisses personal spiritual development as unimportant, which in turn means the individual's faith journey "hasn't kept pace with their [sic] emotional, intellectual, and moral development."[8] This results in adults functioning with a childish understanding of faith and the spiritual journey.

In her book, *Big Questions, Worthy Dreams: Mentoring Emerging Adults in Their Search for Meaning, Purpose, and Faith,* Sharon Daloz Parks makes a strong case for the development of faith as a major component of becoming a mature adult. She speaks of faith as *"the activity of making-meaning in the most comprehensive dimensions of our awareness."*[9] Although John Lennon, with his 1971 ballad "Imagine," famously popularized the sentiment that getting rid of all religion would make the world a better place, the reality on the ground is that religion is not an accident of the

5. See Davie, *Religion in Britain.*

6. Bass, *Christianity after Religion.*

7. McLennan, *Finding Your Religion,* 98.

8. McLennan, *Finding Your Religion,* 15.

9. Parks, *Big Questions, Worthy Dreams,* x (italics hers).

human imagination but a framework though which humans can make meaning and mature as spiritual beings.

Perhaps we are seeing a reluctance of all sides to listen carefully to the Other for how we might all move forward in wisdom and love and understanding. Perhaps we need to step back and look again at what the world faiths actually believe: the core principles and why they were established—core principles such as love and peace, justice and joy, harmony and understanding. We need to give ourselves and each other permission to reexamine the subsequent layers of tradition that have accumulated and balance them against these core principles. We need to listen carefully to each other across the faith boundaries, not holding up the worst in any tradition as justification for its vilification but encouraging the best from each. In this way we all can learn from each other and contribute toward a closer binding of us all into the ways of peace and love and understanding that we all crave.

CHAPTER 3

When Hearts Join and Faiths Collide

EASTER SUNDAY A FEW years ago found me on a beach in Thailand, ready to begin the wedding blessing ceremony for one of our foster daughters and her fiancé. She had been born into the Zoroastrian faith, educated at Christian schools, and practiced Buddhism in recent years. Her fiancé's mother was Hindu and his father Swiss Catholic; he was somewhat ambivalent about both faith traditions. They had asked me several months previously if I would conduct the wedding blessing. At the time, I was living in London and they were living in Singapore, but we had several online sessions in which we worked through the wedding details.

At one point I emailed them a heavily edited copy of the British Methodist wedding liturgy to consider. They returned it with all the prayers and Scripture readings deleted. The initial greeting of my suggested liturgy remained: we were gathered to celebrate the love they shared and to ask for blessings on their marriage from God and their friends and family. I gently asked how I was to invoke God's blessing if I could not pray or read Scripture in the service. They agreed that *I* could pray and read a Scripture, but they did not want to offend the various religious sensibilities of their guests, so no one would be expected to join in any prayers or religious readings.

As I stood on that sunny Thai beach, I had a twinge of guilt remembering my British congregation shivering at the Easter service back in London. Then I saw the hundred-plus wedding guests gathered from all parts of the world—investment bankers, entrepreneurs, Bollywood producers—and another hundred guests from the resort looking on, as there was no other entertainment available for the afternoon. I decided John Wesley, the

22

founder of Methodism who had been advised to "be more vile" in finding ways to address people in their natural settings, would be content with my Easter "congregation," perhaps none of whom would have been at any religious venue that day.

The ceremony proceeded with vows made amidst the sun and sand. My prayers were augmented by the groom's aunties singing a Hindu *bhajan* as they garlanded the couple. After the ceremony, several young men, individually and very discretely, sought me out to say how much they had appreciated the service. "We go to many weddings these days, but this one was different. There was something sacred here, and there is hardly ever room for the sacred in our lives today."

There is hardly ever room for the sacred in our lives today.

The wistfulness of that phrase spoke to me not only of the wholesale abandonment of religion in much of today's world, but also of the uncertainty of how to interact with people of diverse faith traditions. We don't know how to talk to each other about religion and faith anymore. The massive globalization of the world over the past few decades has made us vaguely aware that the Other brings different traditions and different gifts to this conversation about how we connect with the divine and each other, but we don't seem to have the language to talk about it with each other. Sometimes we have prejudged the other on the basis of too little knowledge, sometimes we have avoided the conversation for fear of offending. Very often we have thought it best to simply avoid the conversation at all costs. But that approach has cost us dearly indeed. We have lost the conversation about the things that connect us most intimately.

Theologian Wesley Ariarajah, former World Council of Churches Deputy General Secretary for Dialogue with People of Other Faiths, has said it this way: there is a great need for all faith groups to work together rather than in opposition. "[M]ost important today is the knowledge, acknowledgment and acceptance that there are different foundations on which societies are organized, and that none of them has been able to produce the ideal society . . . Perhaps we have much to learn from one another's experiences."[1]

Interfaith marriage is one place where we can begin to have those conversations. We will need resources and tools for our discussions. We will need trust and respect to have the conversations well. We will need support

---

1. Ariarajah, *Not without My Neighbour*, 17–18.

from our communities to continue when the conversations get difficult. But we need the conversations.

Growth of Interfaith Marriage

Ironically, while the institutions of marriage and religion show signs of decline, the rate of interfaith marriage has grown enormously over recent decades. Actual figures for interfaith marriages are hard to find, in part because many governments no longer record the faith tradition of those getting married, especially in civil ceremonies. Some estimates for the US approach 50 percent[2]; and interfaith marriages in UK and Western Europe have grown massively since the days when Protestant-Catholic unions were first furtively ventured. When I tentatively inquired with the chaplain of a large university in South India about whether interfaith marriage was an issue on that campus, he immediately responded saying interest was *huge*.

Globalization has played a major part in the increase of interfaith marriages, providing opportunities for people to get to know a wider variety of potential spouses. As Mary Helene and Ned Rosenbaum, a Catholic/Jewish couple, note: "Our society is too mobile, too fluid, too unprotecting to make it possible for people to stay out of acquaintance and out of love."[3] The change of social assumptions about marriage—from a family/tribal-based union based on regulation of sexual activity to a love-based institution—and changes in how society regards religion—questioning and redefining what belief and practice are about—have also played into the growth of interfaith and mixed-belief unions. The progressive question is not about how we stop this from happening but how we can support the conversation possibilities that occur.

Challenges to Exogamy

Traditionally, most, if not all, religious groups have rejected exogamy, the technical word for interfaith or mixed-belief marriage. Nearly all faith groups have encouraged—or demanded—their community members to stick to their own kind when seeking a marriage partner. Of course, the very fact that exogamy is so often mentioned indicates its prevalence! In

2. Riley, *'Til Faith Do Us Part*, 6.
3. Rosenbaum and Rosenbaum, *Celebrating Our Differences*, iii.

part two of this book, we'll look in more depth at beliefs and practices of specific faith traditions and some of the reasons for discouraging marrying out. These are often based on fear of the Other, especially apparent in groups with histories of persecution from others.[4]

While the perceived threat of interfaith marriage has been around for ages, its modern incidence first emerged with Catholic-Protestant unions in the nineteenth and early twentieth centuries. Prior to the Protestant Reformation a few centuries before, both these groups were simply Christian, so the question arises as to whether the later objections arose from a perceived need to distinguish between competing belief systems.

The Catholic-Protestant unions were followed by a growth in Christian-Jewish marriages as Jewish exiles from the Holocaust arrived in Western Europe and the USA, even though such marriages had been specifically banned for Christians in 306 CE.[5] Again, the fact that a ban was imposed implies that they were indeed happening. Christian-Jewish marriages still meet today with some rejection, the most extreme coming from Conservative and Orthodox Jewish communities who label such unions "a nail in Hitler's coffin," that is, a rejection of the tenuous existence of a persecuted minority. Much has been written about Christian-Jewish marriages; indeed, most of the existing literature on interfaith marriage focuses on such.[6] Contemporary Christian theologian Martin Marty noted that the subsequent exogamous phase (in the US, during the 1990s) consisted of Christians marrying "gnostics [sic] and agnostics, indifferent and somewhat-different,

---

4. Ironically, some faith practices which were intended to restrict exogamous marriages have actually increased them. For instance, Muslim women are forbidden to marry outside of Islam, but the Qur'an allows Muslim men to marry Christians or Jews. While this practice was workable in traditional Muslim societies, when transferred to non-Muslim countries, Muslim women have found themselves lacking suitable marriage partners as considerable numbers of Muslim males have married out. Subsequently, Muslim women are increasingly defying religious restrictions and marrying out as well (Rosenbaum and Rosenbaum, *Celebrating Our Differences*, 123).

5. Romain, *Till Faith Us Do Part*, 22.

6. See especially Miller, *Being Both*, as well as Riley, *'Til Faith Do Us Part*; Romain, *Till Faith Us Do Part*; Rosenbaum and Rosenbaum, *Celebrating Our Differences*; and Seamon, *interfaith marriage in America*. It is interesting to note that each of these authors, while exploring the virtues of interfaith marriage (including their own) and the potential for personal and familial spiritual development with such marriages, ultimately advises against exogamy.

non-observant semiobservants [sic]."[7] The most recent trend in interfaith marriage research literature has dealt with Christian-Muslim unions.[8]

The current wave of exogamous relations in the Western world involves Hindus, Sikhs, and Jains from the Indian subcontinent; such unions are also growing within India, though at a slower pace. Within Hinduism, the specter of marrying out involves not only religious but also caste prohibitions, which permeate the whole of the social fabric. Hindus, not surprisingly in this respect, are the "least likely to marry some of a different religion."[9] At the same time, the changing realities of contemporary society mean that religious prohibitions are often being ignored. As one beleaguered Indian father put it: "When it is time to marry your son . . . , caste is the first thought that goes through your mind. Pretty soon, you realize it's not going to work . . . you think, any girl from Tamilnadu [sic] is OK, then any girl from South India is OK, then any girl from India is OK, then, finally, you say *any* good girl is OK."[10]

Working Out the Differences

While the prohibitions abound, digging deeper into religious belief systems also reveals affirmation for interfaith marriage, albeit scanty at times, in nearly all faith traditions. My interest is not in deciding whether creedal opposition to interfaith marriage from faith communities is justified; I am more concerned with recognizing that interfaith marriage is a contemporary phenomenon from which both faith traditions and interfaith families could benefit by considering how best to support each other. Rather than rejecting those who are questioning the traditions, rather than rejecting all religion because of specific incidents, rather than assigning blame, rather than making assumptions about those who are different, we need to find ways of listening to and talking through faith issues with others.[11]

7. Marty, quoted in Seamon, *interfaith marriage in America*, 163.

8. See Richmond, *Blessed and Called*; Scott and Warren, *Perspectives on Marriage*; Riley, *'Til Faith Do Us Part*; and Miller, *Being Both*.

9. Pew Forum on Religion and Public Life, *U.S. Religious Landscape Survey*, 34.

10. Sutherland, "Wedding Pavilion," 125 (italics original).

11. A certain linguistic irony arises in that the contemporary search for a soul mate as a marriage partner blithely ignores the previous assumption that a faith community (or its leaders) might be an appropriate place to look for a God-ordained soul mate (Riley, *'Til Faith Do Us Part*, 44).

When interfaith marriage works well, it offers encouragement to a world which struggles with peaceful interactions with the Other. Those who undertake it are often idealistic persons finding union with other such idealists; they see themselves as showing that love overcomes differences. The strapline for my project on interfaith marriage, "Working for world peace at the most intimate level," met with some reluctance from several interfaith couples I worked with. They were reluctant to ascribe to such a massive undertaking, but an interfaith husband in another study came to this conclusion: "What we were doing amounted to *a model for world peace! I figured if we could live together with relatively low friction on this very divisive* [interfaith] *issue, there was hope for the Israelis and Palestinians.*"[12]

Indeed, many of those who marry out have valuable contributions to make to the interfaith conversation. Rather than abandoning their faith traditions, exogamists often take their faith seriously, so seriously that they are attracted to potential partners who also take their own faith seriously, even when their partner's faith is not their own. Some are attracted to a religious partner because they are consciously or unconsciously seeking to learn more about religious faith. Some are testing or prodding tenets of their own religion: beliefs such as hospitality, equality, love and respect for the stranger, or world peace. Often those willing to commit themselves to a long-term relationship with a person from a different background are persons with strong commitments to values such as honoring diversity and working for the common good.

What Faith Traditions Have to Offer

The statistics for *successful* interfaith marriages are very mixed, with some sources claiming three times as many interfaith marriages end in divorce than marriages in general. Others claim the divorce rates are virtually the same. Critics of interfaith marriage are quick to claim that *successful* marriages can only emerge from couples with similar faith backgrounds. Still others suggest that such conclusions do not deal with the essential problem of how to negotiate diversity.

Naomi Schaefer Riley conducted a survey in the USA in 2012 in which she explored issues of marital satisfaction amongst couples of different religious and political backgrounds. Overall, 80 percent of the couples

---

12. Wernick, quoted in Dale McGowan, *In Faith and In Doubt*, 198 (italics original).

which she surveyed indicated a high level of marital satisfaction.[13] Riley went on to compare statistics of interfaith couples with those from same-faith or no-faith marriages and found that marital satisfaction was almost always higher for same-faith couples. Her further investigations suggested a link between marital satisfaction and personal spiritual growth, in turn suggesting that personal spiritual growth is more difficult for a married couple following different faith traditions.

Intrigued by Ms Riley's study, I conducted a similar survey in early 2018 with alumni from the international school in India where I worked for many years. The responses I received from students (currently living in more than two dozen countries) revealed a higher rate of marital satisfaction than in Riley's survey reported: 92 percent satisfaction rate overall, with an 85 percent satisfaction rate for interfaith couples. This observation prompted me to consider that this high rate of marital satisfaction could be a by-product of the school's high regard for intercultural and interfaith relationships, an emphasis especially enforced through the school's residential program in which students are intentionally exposed to ways of dealing with differences in their everyday interactions.

In my survey, the link between marital satisfaction and spiritual maturity became even more apparent as those who were most *dissatisfied* with their interfaith marriages were also those who considered themselves to be Nones (no religious faith claimed) or atheists, that is, they considered themselves nonbelievers and/or did not presently identify with a faith community. Marital dissatisfaction was very high (93 percent) for those who experienced at least some rejection from their families when they chose to marry out. In many cases, this family rejection would have been on religious grounds, thus providing a reason for the one facing rejection to in turn reject his/her birth religion. A higher percentage of those who were dissatisfied with their interfaith marriage (35 percent compared with 23 percent of the general responses) also reported no support for their marriage, either from family, friends, or a faith tradition. Comparing the difference between levels of marital satisfaction for couples who receive support from a faith community and those who do not suggests that such support can nurture not only spiritual growth but also, in turn, enhance marital satisfaction.

13. Riley, *Til Faith Do Us Part*, 126.

Need for Supportive Faith Community

A gathering of interfaith couples in London invited me to reflect with them in their meeting one Sunday afternoon. They related that most of them had, early in their relationship with their interfaith partner, recognized many shared values, such as the importance of family, fairness, kindness, and honesty. Many of them had also experienced being rejected by their families and/or faith communities and thus finding support cut off, often at the time when they needed it most. When adjusting to new life with a partner, or a new home, or a new child, they often found they were on their own. Many saw it as a contemporary reality: faith groups and family members which traditionally would have helped couples through the challenges of married life were no longer available. Their act of gathering together as interfaith couples was one practical way of addressing that need for support. They were developing community amongst themselves.

While developing community is nearly always a helpful way of coping, doing it on their own meant that many of the traditional cross-generational resources that would have been available to them were in fact missing. Resources such as premarital and marital counseling and training from faith leaders, which has been common in many faith traditions, has rarely been offered to those marrying out of their faith tradition. While the interfaith couples gathered that day seemed committed to each other and their marriages, many seemed to have only vague ideas of the importance of their own spiritual journeys or the communal support these require. Instead, there was a certain sense of loneliness and improvisation which could be exhausting in the long run.

As the interfaith couples seemed generally resigned to making their marriages work on their own, I was reminded of McLennan's observations about the contemporary attempt to make the spiritual journey an individual rather than a communal activity. He offers the analogy of the spiritual journey as a mountain-climbing endeavor: "You might be tempted to avoid any of the well-trodden paths, but bushwhacking usually doesn't get you very far, especially if you are an inexperienced climber."[14] Climbing the mountain is considerably easier with an experienced guide, and the journey is much more enjoyable in the company of others. The *ligare*[15] of religion becomes the guide rope which provides security for individuals

14. McLennan, *Finding Your Religion*, 67.

15. The Latin word *ligare* is the root of the word "religion."

bound together on a spiritual journey. Indeed, marriage itself can be an important aspect of one's spiritual journey: faith communities do well to consider how they will support spiritual journeys within interfaith marriages.

The present conversation between faith communities and the young (or even middle-aged adults) is often tentative at best, so hospitality to interfaith couples could provide an opportunity to strengthen or even create new links between young adults and faith communities. As the Methodist church (and others) seek to reverse the exit tide of Emerging Adults who feel traditional faith communities have nothing to offer—and considering that many of these young adults are involved in interfaith relationships—I challenge my own Methodist church to find meaningful ways of supporting and interacting with interfaith couples. While it's generally observed that more than 50 percent of those marrying out will leave their own faith community, growing evidence also indicates that those who marry out often have a high regard for religious faith.[16] Indeed, several authors report that many of those in interfaith marriages become *more* religious,[17] perhaps indicating a conscious or unconscious challenge to their religious communities' understandings of hospitality and acceptance. These couples could provide helpful conversation partners for churches who are also praying and seeking for ways to work for world peace.

British Methodist Perspective

In 1999, the British Methodist Conference issued a statement on interfaith relations as part of its larger document, "Called to Love and Praise":

> The Church's vocation is to be a sign, witness, foretaste and instrument of God's kingdom . . . engaging with people of differing cultures and religious faiths . . . Christians of all traditions are at the beginning of a long period of growing dialogue with people of other faiths. To refuse opportunities for such dialogue would be a denial of both tolerance and Christian love. To predict, at this point in time, the outcome of such dialogue would be presumptuous or faithless; Christians may enter such dialogues in the faith that God will give them deeper insight into the truth of Christ.[18]

16. Birtwistle, "Water Mixed with Wine," 10, 15, 70, 186.

17. Miller, *Being Both*; Richmond, *Blessed and Called*; Rosenbaum and Rosenbaum, *Celebrating Our Differences*.

18. Trustees for Methodist Church Purposes, "Called to Love and Praise," 16–17.

Here hospitality is identified as a primary resource and means of participating in God's mission in the world. It is important to recognize this mission not solely in terms of potential conversions into Christianity but rather in terms of learning and growing together spiritually. Methodist interfaith proponent Elizabeth Harris observes that congregations are often theologically more eager to welcome those who are unchurched or atheist than those who come from other faiths.[19] Still, the British Methodist "law book" (*Constitutional Practice and Discipline*) also recognizes the potential of interfaith discussion in the marital situation:

> All faiths cherish marriage and most would agree that seeking God's blessing on marriage is vital. In Britain's pluralist society, there are more and more opportunities for marriage between people of different faiths. There are some who would see this as a cause for celebration, for it can betoken the meeting of faiths at a very deep social level, that of the life of the family.[20]

John Wesley's famous saying, "If your heart is as my heart, *give me your hand*," reminds us that the joining of hearts and hands is at the core of most wedding ceremonies. Interfaith marriage thus seems an ideal place for the faith community to invite young adults into mutual conversations about what constitutes a faith journey, a spiritual journey, and an opportunity to grow with each other as spiritual persons.

19. Harris, *Theology and use*, 2.

20. Trustees for Methodist Church Purposes, "Guidelines for Inter-Faith Marriages," 2:800–802.

CHAPTER 4

Tools for Crossing Boundaries and Nurturing Growth

I WAS TRAVELING BY train to London from a conference in Manchester where I had been presenting some of my initial findings on interfaith marriage. The train was running late, and the reserved seating arrangements were in upheaval, so, as the train pulled out of the station, I plopped down in the last available seat, next to quiet and serious young man. As I settled in and picked up my knitting, we slowly began to chat.

He was from a Romanian Orthodox (Christian) background, married to an English woman whose parents were Methodists and had taught in Arabia and Pakistan. The couple were living in London with their one-year-old son and, in his words, not practicing any religion. He was very dismissive of the Orthodox faith which he felt was based on strict doctrine with little room for questioning. As I gently engaged him in conversation about his best childhood faith memory, he spoke solemnly about the mystic joy of joining in the nighttime Easter vigil in his village, how the priest had led them singing through the darkness from house to welcoming house. I ventured further to inquire of his worst childhood faith memory, and he spoke of his confusion and dismay when the same village priest had later refused to perform his wedding to his non-Orthodox fiancée. Those memories lingering, we talked about the importance of having a faith tradition in one's life and of being able to think it through and push back at the parts that didn't make sense. We spoke gently of the importance of passing faith traditions on to his child, so that the child would have some knowledge when it came time for him to choose a faith for himself.

When the train journey finished (an hour late!), he thanked me profusely for a "most interesting conversation" and then ran down the station platform with a joyful spring in his trot. It reminded me of the story in John's Gospel of the woman at the well who ran away from her conversation with Jesus in eagerness to tell others about how she'd been heard and energized to understand her faith in a new way.

One does not usually talk to strangers on the train from Manchester to London, much less engage in what amounts to marital counseling. (Perhaps my knitting rendered me safe.) One does take whatever opportunities one has to engage in conversations that might lead to world peace; the conversation on the train is one that can be helpful for all interfaith couples. Many of the techniques for that conversation came from the world of marriage counseling.

Counseling is one of the tools that faith leaders traditionally learned and used regularly with couples preparing to marry, but it has, like the institutions of marriage and religion, fallen out of favor with contemporary society. Just as many think religion tells you what to believe, so many consider that counselors tell you what to do. In reality, a good personal counselor will help one discover and explore oneself, and a good marriage counselor will help a couple each explore better ways of understanding themselves and fostering good communication.

Since most interfaith couples will resist "counseling," I have learned to call my sessions "marriage workshops." An even more attractive option has been to offer couples an opportunity to be part of "doctoral research" as everyone seems to think their own situation would provide useful insights for others. One such couple who agreed to do a few sessions was astounded when I finally revealed that we had been doing marriage counseling. They exclaimed in wide-eyed wonder, "Everyone should do this!" The challenge remains in how to graciously offer such tools so that they can be used and embraced.

From the interfaith marriage perspective, counseling can address two main challenges: (1) how to navigate and negotiate a marriage over the long-term, and (2) how to address interfaith issues, recognizing that sometimes these are more accurately intercultural issues. Though it is tempting to assume that any challenge to an interfaith marriage will center on faith issues, experience reveals that negotiating the marriage tasks comes first.

In any relationship, each will need to learn the language of the other in order to establish effective communication. In any marriage, each needs to learn to recognize the unconscious assumptions that s/he brings into the marriage and how to negotiate them. That negotiation process is made more difficult as many interfaith couples become isolated, pushed away from the support of their families of origin and/or their faith community who otherwise might give them stories and space to help make sense of unconscious assumptions. Even when interfaith couples want the premarital or marriage counseling that many faith communities traditionally offered, it is rarely available to them. A new workable model is needed to help interfaith couples build successful marriages and become spiritually mature persons. This would include:

- developing general skills in recognizing and resolving marital conflict;

- exploring theologies of marriage and spiritual maturity in each spouse's faith traditions, and how to respect and negotiate differences in the traditions;

- promoting an eagerness for individual and mutual spiritual maturity, including family life, raising children in a life of faith, and mending broken or strained relationships with birth families and/or in-laws.

The brave couples who agreed to help with my research also contributed many insights. Nearly all found the tools presented helpful. One couple reflected that while ultimately each couple would have to develop strategies and agreements for themselves, they valued having "dedicated time and space to think about those things" as well as "someone to bounce off of . . . to get a different perspective and more tools for discussion." Still another couple resisted interaction throughout all the sessions until the groom-to-be arrived one morning to pick up a final bit of documentation that he'd requested. Suddenly his eyes clouded over as he whispered, "I didn't realize how much all this would mean to me." We are all stronger when we can support each other and allow ourselves to be supported.

Recognizing Roots: Expectations from Childhood

A basic tenet of marital counseling is that we each unconsciously learn about gender roles, family dynamics, relationships, and values from our families of origin. The ancient taboo against incest ensures that virtually every marriage involves persons who grew up in different households and with somewhat different expectations for family, and that every marriage will encounter diversity of some sort. Recognizing where each has come from is a crucial first step toward working out how one will negotiate and grow in the liminal boundary state between family patterns and expectations, the place between cultures, traditions, and beliefs: the place where interfaith couples most often reside.

Dealing with diverse childhood experiences is a firmly established strategy for marital and premarital counseling; it is essential for the successful flourishing of interfaith marriage. One might assume that everyone's mother makes the morning tea until one spends the night in a home where Dad (or Grandma or Nan or an older sibling or even a family servant) is the early riser who gets food on the breakfast table—or perhaps there is no breakfast. The patterns and roles we learn in our childhood homes become the standards by which we subsequently and usually unconsciously judge the rest of the world. They become the basis for how we understand ourselves and others. Assumptions are implanted early about who can or should make money, about how it is to be spent and who spends it, about who works inside and/or outside the home, and how the family relates to its community. Our childhood families present us with norms for how to raise, educate, and discipline children, how intimacy is expressed or shared within the home, and how nuclear families relate to their wider extended families. They set our expectations for how we will celebrate and regard religion and faith development.

As we mature, we learn that there are multiple ways of living with others, even as we harbor our own expectations of how things are to be done the right way. Inevitably a marriage involves negotiating the space between two right ways, which in turn becomes an opportunity for blending together two sets of assumptions and coming up with new ways of doing and being. As such, the intimacy of marriage is one of most important vehicles (along with parenting) by which we humans learn to negotiate through the conflict and so grow as persons.

Interfaith marriages seemingly reject the time-honored wisdom which dictates that by marrying someone of a similar family background, less conflicts will need to be resolved. An interfaith marriage has the potential—and responsibility—to take this intimate conflict resolution even further as the faith component becomes an opportunity to explore the benefits and liabilities, strengths and weaknesses, insights and blind spots of whole religions and faith traditions. We will explore that further in the next chapter, though noting that interfaith marriage researcher Susan Katz

35

Miller claims: "interfaith couples actually enter marriage with advantages, even if they face opposition. Through their choice of partner, they have demonstrated open-mindedness and a willingness to listen and cooperate, important skills in remaining married."[1] She also quotes an interfaith-friendly minister who has noted, "Interfaith couples work much harder and more intentionally on their marriages."[2]

Interfaith marriage experts Patrice E. Heller and Beatrice Wood note differences in what same-faith and interfaith couples bring to the marriage discussion:

> Intramarried couples [that is, from the same faith tradition] appear to experience greater personal similarity and mutual understanding rooted in their ethnic bond, which aids the development of intimacy. Intermarried couples appear to find that the very process of negotiating ethnic differences leads to great mutual understanding and intimacy.[3]

In that respect, confronting difference becomes an opportunity for personal and mutual growth. But it is not easy.

Tools for Dealing with Conflict

General marriage counseling uses conflict management tools for dealing with deep-rooted marital conflicts. It recognizes that the roots of conflict have often been planted in one's childhood when rational processes are just beginning to form. As such, the conflict roots are stored as "feelings," often termed "reptilian" in conflict management-speak. But these conflict roots can also resemble the innocent-looking nettle plants that flourish in the British countryside; they are innocent only until one accidentally brushes against them and is inflicted with a fierce and lasting sting. A diligent gardener will seek to grasp the nettles, pulling them out from their roots; a more tolerant gardener might leave the nettles in their place but keep an eye out for the accompanying dock plant which counteracts the sting and usually grows nearby. Successful marriage partners learn to recognize the nettles of feeling rooted deeply in their own and their partner's childhood experiences, nettles which can sprout unexpectedly, especially in the heat

---

1. Miller, *Being Both*, 82.
2. Rev. Jarvis, quoted in Miller, *Being Both*, 82.
3. Heller and Wood, "Influence of Religious and Ethnic Differences," 241.

of disagreement. They learn to recognize and regard each other's feelings as facts which are to be respected within in the relationship, even if they are not equally shared by both. Wise couples also learn how to use the dock tools to listen, respect, negotiate, and respond so that the stings are healed, so that each one wins or, even better, so that the couple wins and grows together.

In counseling sessions with interfaith couples, each is asked to separately complete a questionnaire about his/her birth family.[4] These help us begin to identify the discrepancies they have each inherited from their childhood. As with feelings being facts, there are no right or wrong ways to respond to questions about when and where and how a family eats or sleeps or worships or celebrates together. Each family unit will have developed different ways of interacting with each other. If one received a set allowance or pocket money each week, that one will regard money differently than one who had to work for any spending money or one who was given whatever s/he asked for. If one's parents made a point of never arguing in front of the children, one develops different expectations than those of a family whose practice was to debate anything and everything openly and loudly.

Once the discrepancies are identified, the discussions can begin, but often couples—like much of our society—lack the tools for discussing. They're usually intrigued to hear about having a "fair fight,"[5] and these techniques become an important tool for working through their discrepancies. "Fair fight" is often the favorite activity for those in counseling sessions. First and foremost, it involves learning how to listen carefully to the other and how to respond effectively, ensuring that both parties know they have been heard. In a fair fight, each takes responsibility for his/her own actions and reactions, striving to use "I" statements rather than accusatory "you" statements. Any form of violence to make one's point is prohibited, which helps ensure that the disagreement has a chance of being resolved in a safe arena.

The real fun begins when the ground rules are put into practice. In a counseling session, the counselor acts as the referee for the practice round, with the couple identifying an issue on which they are currently disagreeing.[6] These fights consist of alternating rounds, each lasting approximately

4. See Appendix 2.

5. Cobb, "Fair Fighting Rules for Couples."

6. In refereeing nearly all the initial fair fights, I needed to gently remind the couple to address *each other* rather than me when they were presenting or responding.

two minutes, during which one spouse is the Presenter and the other the Listener. The Fair Fights are often deeply revealing. The couple who decided to fight about who empties the dishwasher and when it is to be done began to recognize that they were operating on different assumptions about not only male/female roles but about standards of housekeeping and the value of "housework" versus "real work" (their labels).

One couple recognized that she had better verbal skills than he, so it was easier for her to win the arguments, though in reality, the disagreements were just buried deeper in his resentment of both losing the argument and being unable to put his view forward. When she learned to listen more deeply and make adequate space for him to learn to speak, their communication improved, and resentments were eased. Both were able to grow as they learned to see each other from the other's position.

Taking time to have a refereed fair fight can also reveal deeper issues. One couple's fight about her habit of leaving the TV on all day revealed his anxiety about wasting money and hers about growing up alone as an only child. Each began to realize they were looking for security in different forms: in money or in companionship. Another couple approached their disagreement about how to treat their newly adopted cat as an illustration of their different understandings about respect for animals. Part-way into their fair fight, he retorted, "But he [the cat] deserves to be treated as a person!" At that they both stopped short, eyes opened wide, mouths shut, realizing they were really venturing into a discussion about child-raising, an issue they had avoided previously as they sensed their diverse faith backgrounds would not agree.

It's often assumed that all disagreements in interfaith marriages will center on faith issues. Virtually all couples have disputes about power or sex or money, issues that have deep roots in our childhood expectations. The Rosenbaums, an intermarried Christian/Jewish couple, warn against masking these disputes as simply faith issues. Faith differences can complicate the issues, but the Rosenbaums advise: "leave the theology till you're cooler and talk about the real controversy."[7]

Once good communication and negotiation skills are in place, interfaith couples are better equipped to deal with the issues that their differing faith backgrounds bring to the relationship. If at some point they begin to recognize that perhaps some of their assumptions about gender roles actually *are* based on their diverse faith background, the discussion can be

---

7. Rosenbaum and Rosenbaum, *Celebrating Our Differences*, 65.

about the assumptions of those religious practices rather than the integrity of one's spouse. That is the place where even more interesting discussions can begin.

Tools for the Marital Interfaith Dialogue

Part two of this book provides wide-stroke overviews of several faith traditions to point interfaith couples toward better understandings of each other's perhaps subconscious faith roots. Though some might want to distance themselves from the faith traditions of their birth family, inevitably these practices and perhaps unconscious beliefs still function at some deep level of expectations established in childhood. In the counseling workshops, each couple is required to read the chapters that pertain both to the faith tradition of his/her own family and that of his/her spouse. They are asked to note questions they will want to discuss in sessions and privately with their spouse—or perhaps even research further on their own.

The materials in part two are intentionally limited in scope: it takes at least a lifetime for any of us to explore and learn all there is about a particular faith tradition, so no single chapter can possibly provide all the information needed for a lifetime journey. The part-two explorations do focus on a few of the key questions that impact on marriage and marriage relationships, especially marriage as a vehicle for personal and mutual spiritual maturity: How and why are humans created? How are gender roles approached? What does spiritual maturity look like from this faith perspective? Having noted the importance of faith issues absorbed unconsciously from childhood, there are "Aha!" moments even for those whose parents had formally or informally discarded religious belief, moments when family traditions, aversions, or habits suddenly make some sense.

A Christian/Muslim couple were eager to discuss and question their part-two readings. She, an English woman engaged to a Bangladeshi Muslim, was a little uneasy with finding some aspects of Islam that she had tried to explain/defend to others ignorant of Islam were actually part of the Qur'an; he was quick to point out the difficulty of using only the Qur'an (and not Sunnah and Hadith—later sayings of Muhammad and scholarly interpretations) as a primary source. She was also interested in reading about how understandings of marriage and gender had changed from the Old Testament to the New. He expressed frustration that "Christianity has been allowed to grow, but Islam cannot change"; he understood this to be a result of the fixed nature of Muhammad's received revelation. He was eager to find others who, like he, were trying to seriously practice the principles of Islam, while also accommodating the realities of living in a secularized, scientifically informed world.

Three Titles: A Tool for
Exploration of Personal Faith Roots

The conversation techniques the young man and I engaged with on the train journey at the beginning of this chapter grew out of an exercise called "Three Titles," which I had encountered in another setting and then developed to help interfaith couples identify and explore issues of faith arising from their childhood experiences. It builds on the Presenter (Storyteller) and Listener roles introduced in previous workshop sessions.

In my version, the Presenter offers three titles of short stories about *positive faith* incidents from his/her childhood. The Listener chooses to hear one of stories behind the three titles, listens carefully, and then reports back what has been heard. The Presenter and Listener roles are then reversed. A second round of storytelling follows featuring three *negative* faith incidents from each. Because listening techniques featured prominently in the earlier sessions, this exercise provides couples opportunities to share their childhood *faith* experiences through personal stories they can explore together. As before, a counselor can help the couple identify and clarify issues in the session through careful listening. By only using one of the titles in each category during our session, the couple will potentially have several other stories to explore together later.

Many couples have found that Three Titles gave them a new space to explore their varied faith backgrounds. One couple consisted of an Anglo-Indian woman, who had come from a staunch Christian background, and her Indian husband, whose family had parted from a Hindu tradition and become "free-thinkers" (his term). Both presented themselves as agnostic at the beginning of our sessions, but by the end of the Three Titles exercise—in which their positive faith stories reminded them of communal bonds no longer functioning in their current lives—they were both eager to learn about the faith traditions they (or their families) had set aside. He seriously suggested they should start attending church together with their young daughter so she would also have a taste of a communal faith experience.

Sharing the negative faith stories was important for another Muslim/ Christian couple who realized they both had memories in which a male figure whom they admired (her father, his religious education teacher) had refused to have a conversation with them about a particular faith issue. At the time, they had been confused at the silencing on faith issues. They both realized they were still eager to have such conversations and grateful to have had the opportunity to spend significant time during our sessions discussing faith questions.

Another couple's Three Titles exercise revealed stories from their teenage years in which each of them had (1) encountered persons who were positively assertive about their faith, and (2) discovered that a big-topic issue for society in general—Islamophobia and sexism—became a deeply personal experience for themselves or someone close to them. They recognized that each of these situations informed the way they were conducting their personal faith journeys, their interfaith relationship, and their upcoming marriage.

None of these techniques and exercises— identifying discrepancies in childhood experiences, conflict resolution methods, fair fights, reading and learning about faith traditions, sharing stories through Three Titles—are a guarantee for happy ever after, but each can be an important tool for learning to negotiate the liminal space of an interfaith marriage.

CHAPTER 5

Posing the Hard Questions

THE YOUNG INDIAN WOMAN sitting across from me had been a childhood friend of my daughter decades earlier when we lived and worked in South India. They had played "House-House" and "Dr. Barbie Gets Married" on our front veranda. Her parents had been colleagues of ours at the international school. Now an articulate professional herself, K was relating the story of her own interfaith marriage which, sadly, had not been happy ever after.

K had met her husband-to-be while they were both studying in university in India. They were just friends at first, aware of their religious differences: she was a practicing Catholic and he a Hindu. In time, their friendship developed, and they decided to get married. Her parents initially advised against the marriage, though they themselves were somewhat of an interfaith couple, having come from Roman Catholic and Protestant backgrounds. After an extended engagement, her parents agreed on the condition that there would be no dowry, a stipulation common with nearly all Christian traditions in India. K and her fiancé agreed to respect each other's religious differences and that neither would be required to convert to the other's religion. They then sought in vain to find a priest who would marry them, finally opting for a civil ceremony.

After their wedding, K moved with her husband into his family home where she soon realized she was expected to participate in religious traditions and abide by religious restrictions that were at odds with her own beliefs. K's husband also became more mentally and emotionally unstable, subjecting her to emotional abuse. Soon after their son was born, K recognized the extent of their differences and the abuse she was receiving. She filed for divorce and moved with her son to her parents' home.

During our conversation together, K understood I was researching interfaith marriage and how best to support such couples in their relationship. In K's case, the marriage was no longer salvageable, but I was impressed with her ability to persevere in finding a workable solution to a difficult situation. Hearing her story made me aware again of the contemporary challenges of both marriage and interfaith marriage. I asked if she would consider marrying again. She said yes, but on two conditions: her husband must be good at heart, and he must accept her son. K also said she would contemplate an interfaith marriage again and would encourage others to do the same, but she gave three pieces of advice: (1) Consider what support you will have; your own parents' support is essential. (2) Do some research into the other's faith—beliefs and practices, including family expectations—*before* the marriage. (3) Be aware of the potential for abuse and what signs to look for. It is good advice, far beyond what she learned from playing "House-House" and "Dr. Barbie Gets Married."

Family Support

The "Heart says yes, parents say no" scenario mentioned previously is dangerous territory indeed. At its worst, honor killing carries through on an assumption that anyone daring to defy parental or religious preferences is bringing dishonor on the whole family. Thankfully, most families are willing to at least consider positively what attracted the couple to each other across traditional boundaries instead of automatically assigning motives of ignorance or rebellion or even treachery. Still, parental observations can sometimes recognize potential barriers to marital compatibility, so couples are wise to listen and consider. It is one thing to resolutely stick to what one's heart says, it is still another to follow romanticism to the disastrous conclusion of Romeo and Juliet.

In the previous chapter on counseling, we explored listening techniques that couples could use to better understand each other. Learning to say with openness and sincerity "This is what I hear you saying; have I got this right?" can also be a helpful technique to use with family members. K was blessed to have had a good enough relationship with her own parents that she could be in dialogue with them about matters on which they disagreed.

Sometimes interfaith family disagreements can be about issues that have little to do with faith issues. Other times, prejudices need to be addressed and explored. How to do that sensitively is key to good communication and growth for all. Indeed, the prospect of have someone from outside joining the intimacy one's family can be a mutually growing experience for the whole family. Dale McGowan speaks of the "Aunt Susan Principle" in which entrenched attitudes can be radically changed over time when one encounters a real person from a previously excluded Other group. Personal knowledge can overcome deep-seated prejudice.[1] When the Other becomes part of one's family, the family has the potential to become even stronger and richer. Of course, building bridges across age-old divides does not always work, but it is worth the effort.

K's story also raises an awareness of potential abuse, an issue which knows no religious bounds, though human nature will often want to associate specific cases with particular groups or faith communities. K was careful to delink the abuse she experienced in her marriage from the interfaith dimension, understanding it rather as stemming from an emotional/mental imbalance. Still, she's correct in her insistence that doing the research into the other's faith *before* the marriage is helpful in being able to make the distinctions, rather than assuming that abuse is automatically part and parcel of a particular faith tradition.

K is essentially reminding us that it's important to listen with our heads as well as our hearts, that negotiating new territory is difficult work which requires strong support teams, and that our eagerness to take on the challenge might restrict our ability to adequately assess the risks. Still, she expresses an interest in continuing the challenge of finding ways to make world peace at the most intimate level.

Tackling the Hard Questions

In working for world peace, an interfaith couple has the opportunity to sift through the faith traditions and belief systems which they each bring into the marriage. Each religion consists of intertwined *beliefs and practices* which are sometimes nearly impossible to separate out. Indeed, often traditions of local culture—which may or may not have religious roots—dictate that the same religion may be practiced in very different ways with people who come from different areas. For instance, the Christian culture that

1. Dale McGowan, *In Faith and in Doubt,* 203.

I subconsciously learned growing up in the USA had several differences from the Christian culture of South India where I lived as a young adult. African Muslims are different from Indonesian Muslims, and British Buddhists often differ in their practices from those in Nepal. Many cultures are themselves composites of several faith traditions. Chinese culture, for example, which currently considers itself atheist, is strongly influenced by Confucian, Taoist, and Buddhist traditions. It's no easy task to separate out the cultural influences from the strictly religious practices, and, indeed, both culture and religion influence the other.

In this book, we are looking at faith traditions and beliefs particularly as they influence and promote spiritual life and relationships. In this regard, Christian theologian Miroslav Volf and others have pointed out that it is most often the religious *practices* which make the most impact (for better or worse) on our spiritual formation. Volf describes faith practices as "energizing, consoling, healing, liberating, and directing people's lives, giving them meaning" and says that religion in daily life survives "somewhat like the art of cooking thrives not mainly because celebrity chefs display their culinary fireworks on television shows but because mothers and fathers prepare ordinary meals every single day, often more than once, for families and friends."[2] A successful interfaith marriage has to consider carefully how it will honor the faith beliefs and practices which each bring to the marriage.

Andrew Wingate, in his book, *Celebrating Difference, Staying Faithful: How to Live in a Multi-Faith World,* lists several root faith issues interfaith couples will need to negotiate. Apart from the relationships with families of origin and extended families mentioned previously, there are community issues and legal considerations.[3] Again, these may vary according to the particular cultural milieu in which they were experienced, but they each have important implications for negotiating an interfaith marriage.

The emphasis here is on interfaith *marriage,* though similar issues can arise for interfaith couples who are cohabiting. The formalities and legalities of marriage, though, seem to heighten the awareness of faith issues; indeed, the cohabitation arrangement, with its casual assumption that if this doesn't work, we can call it all off, loses some of its care-free abandon when the interfaith/mixed-belief couple decide that they will *marry.* Past all the discussions of readily available divorce, marriage is still *intended* to last for

2. Volf, *Flourishing,* 61.

3. Wingate, *Celebrating Difference,* 129.

the long haul. When an interfaith couple becomes engaged, faith belief/ practice questions arise in earnest.

The first interfaith question that then arises is often "What kind of wedding will we have?," which itself raises issues such as which faith tradition(s) will be followed, and how the couple will honor their diverse faith traditions. Indeed, consideration of possible wedding scenarios provides clues for setting the faith agenda for the rest of the interfaith marriage. Briefly, the wedding possibilities are: .

- One faith tradition will dominate and the wedding ceremony will follow that tradition's practices. This scenario usually assumes (or demands) that one spouse will convert. Sometimes this is symptomatic of a power struggle within the relationship. It may also depend on which faith tradition shows the most acceptance to the couple and especially the one from outside that faith.

- Both spouses will maintain separate faith traditions. The couple will probably either opt for a civil ceremony or have two separate ceremonies.

- Spouses will maintain both faith traditions together. Their wedding will incorporate both faith traditions, and they will each seek to support the other in growing spiritually within their faith tradition.

- The couple will not observe any faith tradition. Usually their wedding will be a civil ceremony.

Each of these has its implications for how the marriage—and the faith development of each—will unfold. Does "one faith will dominate" indicate the other faith will be erased? Does "both maintain separate faith traditions" mean that those traditions are separate but equal? Is the goal of maintaining both faith traditions together actually sustainable? Is the decision to not observe any faith tradition a rejection of faith as an influence in life or an avoidance of difficult territory?

The questions continue for the marriage itself: After the wedding, where/how/when will the couple worship together, or will faith development be ignored? How will religious celebrations such as Christmas or Hanukkah or Diwali be negotiated, if only on a social level? Will there be fasting for Ramadan and/or for Lent? Are the celebrations done at home only, or at a church/temple/mosque? If celebrated outside the home, who is allowed to participate? If one half of the couple is excluded from the religious practices or communal participation, how is the relationship affected?

Even the marriage bed is not a faith-free zone. In her paper, "Negotiating the Interfaith Marriage Bed: Religious Differences and Sexual Intimacies," Samira K. Mehta posits that the contemporary social acceptance of love as the prime motivator for marriage is also accompanied by an assumption that sex will overcome all the difficulties of an interfaith marriage. She counters that "even the nonpracticing interfaith couple may not experience the bedroom as a religion-free zone."[4] What religious scripts about sex have each spouse unconsciously or consciously inherited?

Legal matters also emerge: Are the religious marriage requirements in a particular faith tradition also recognized by the state, i.e., is the marriage legal? Would the marriage be recognized as legal in another country? If the couple moves to another country, do the children's/wife's/husband's legal rights remain? If the couple divorces, often faith traditions (and their legal counterpoints) differ on which spouse is granted custody of the children. In some religions, the husband is entitled to take on more than one wife (especially when the couple does not produce a male offspring). At the death of a spouse, there are different religious practices for how the body is to be disposed of. Some religions deny property rights to the surviving spouse.

Faith questions arise again when the first child is born or even its conception contemplated: In which faith(s) will the child be raised? Will there be a birth or naming ceremony (such as infant baptism or a *bris*)? A coming-of-age ceremony? Will the child receive education in one or more religious faiths? Will s/he be allowed to choose his/her own faith as a teen or young adult?

As the list of issues gets longer, it becomes more essential that an interfaith couple has found ways to recognize and negotiate the different patterns and expectations of faith communities. Finding common ground is a laudable goal in interfaith relationships, but the common ground is more sacred when the uncommon ground has been negotiated. An interfaith marriage provides opportunities for that uncommon ground to be explored together. A couple well-practiced in the fine art of marital dialogue will find these agreements easier to negotiate and have practical tools that enable them to pursue spiritual growth as well.

4. Mehta, "Negotiating the interfaith marriage Bed," 29.

CHAPTER 6

Spiritual Growth within
an Interfaith Marriage

THE LAMENT OF THE young men at the beach wedding, *"There is hardly ever room for the sacred in our lives today,"* sometimes becomes the case for interfaith marriages as well. And yet the ongoing conversation is essential for the well-being of the relationship as well as individual spiritual growth. In previous chapters, we began to explore tools that can enable conversations in interfaith marriages. We'll look now at the four wedding scenarios—one faith will dominate, each will maintain a separate faith tradition, both faith traditions will be maintained together, and no faith tradition will be observed—and how these approaches enable or restrict the sacred conversation in interfaith marriage.

"Not Doing Religion"

The least-promising scenario in terms of marital faith development involves the couple deciding not to observe any faith tradition. The "not religious" stance may seem the most diplomatic and practical alternative, but it can leave the couple spiritually isolated, with virtually no supportive faith community, little support for spiritual growth, and little scope for negotiating the liminal space.[1] Susan Katz Miller urges interfaith couples to seek out

---

1. Dale McGowan, *In Faith and in Doubt,* 251. McGowan argues that the space for negotiation can still be intact in a marriage between a nonbeliever and a person of faith if they intend it to be.

faith communities which will support their spiritual journeys: "Religious community provides intergenerational bonding, the support of wise clergy, preservation of our shared history and texts, and the comfort of ritual—not to mention the arrival of casseroles in times of trouble."[2] I was part of an interfaith panel talking about death and dying with a hospice group when one of the medical practitioners noted that each of our panel members had spoken about how our faith *community* responds to those who are dying or bereaved. She noted that *community* is something the secular world is often desperately seeking.

As noted previously, today's society often dismisses personal spiritual development as unimportant, which results in adults functioning with a childish understanding of faith and the spiritual journey. McLennan adapted the work of Fowler and Oser to describe seven distinct Faith Stages and how God is experienced in each of these. The first of these stages is termed Magic and regards God as all-powerful. The next stage, Reality, begins to recognize a cause-and-effect God. In the third stage, Dependence, God is seen in the role of Protecting Parent. In the ensuing Independence stage, God is often seen as distant; this is also a stage at which atheism is often embraced, usually coinciding with late adolescence and early adulthood. The Interdependence stage recognizes a Paradoxical God who does not sit easily in a particular box or category of belief but is often known in Mystery. The final stage of Unity recognizes an all-pervasive God whose presence is woven through all of life.[3]

McLennan notes that young adults are often in the Independence stage, having left home and occupied themselves with trying to make a life for themselves. They are seeking not only to define their own meaning in life but to find a partner—possibly a life partner—as well. Traditionally, most marriages happen when persons are in the Independent stage of faith development, with young adults working out for themselves whether their childhood religious backgrounds have any meaningful application for their adult lives. For an interfaith couple, the task is compounded by confronting an entirely different set of religious practices and understandings. Or are they so very different? If so, how and why? The liminal perspective prompts questions about how different faith practices impact one's spiritual journey. If an interfaith couple decides to avoid the faith questions altogether, they are in danger of stunting their spiritual developments.

2. Miller, *Being Both*, x.
3. McLennan, *Finding Your Religion*, 20.

Following Separate Paths

More promising than "not doing religion" is the agreement that each will *separately* follow his/her own faith tradition (assuming that each is still allowed to be part of that faith community). The downside is that the outside spouse is often not welcome or included, so faith becomes a private affair, rather than a shared journey. This arrangement might keep the families of origin happy in that neither has lost one of its own, but it can be rather confusing and growth-confining for the couple and their offspring. Similarly, the hands-off approach for children, which assumes the offspring will decide when they're old enough, usually results in considerable confusion later for those teenagers or young adults who have not learned either (or any) faith beliefs or practices.

These two approaches for an interfaith marriage, not doing religion or each pursuing their faith separately, share a common downfall: they preclude the possibility of using the marriage as a tool for mutual spiritual maturity. An interfaith marriage approached as a serious *faith* encounter can enable the journey to move from the Independence stage to the recognition of a Paradoxical God and the possibility for Interdependence. It can be a fertile further space for exploring and encouraging spiritual maturity.

One Faith Will Dominate:
The Place of Conversion in Spiritual Growth

The middle-aged Indian man's face was kind and his manner gentle, but his eyes were sad. A mutual friend, knowing my interest in interfaith marriage, had arranged for us to meet at his home in the bustling South Indian temple city of Madurai. When R arrived, it was late evening, and the steamy heat of the day was gradually cooling. My translator friend Billie and I were exhausted after several hours of journeying, but we wanted to hear R's story.

R met J when they were classmates. R was a Hindu by birth and J came from an evangelical Christian family. They fell in love and decided to marry, though her family raised strong objections based on religious and caste differences. R says of his beloved, "I saw *her*, not the religion," but they frequently discussed religion and decided to wait before marrying. After two and a half years of her family continually finding new reasons for them to delay the marriage, R finally found a church minister willing to marry them, but only on the condition that R first be baptized. R agreed to this, though he says he did not fully understand the implications of the baptism and did not tell his own family. At his baptism, he was given the Christian name, Andrew. The wedding was then conducted privately at the church with a reception a few months later, which his parents attended, though hers refused.

R and J attended church together regularly and he agreed that 10 percent of his income would be given to the church as the tithe. R dutifully tried to share with J in the Christian prayers which he had been given, but he struggled as they were written in a style of Tamil which he found difficult to read and understand. J's brother, an evangelist, then insisted that R was not observing his Christian faith correctly, especially as he still went by his Hindu name instead of Andrew.

Eventually, R had to go to work in Indonesia to support his family, which meant he had to leave his seven-months-pregnant wife behind with her family. Various further work complications arose which meant R was unable to return for his son's birth, which saddened him greatly. Being abroad also meant that R wasn't on hand for legal and cultural rites of passage that accompany a birth. In India, one is born into a faith tradition, so the parents' religion is stated on the baby's birth certificate; R's son's birth certificate listed his parents' religion as Christian, which was technically true. Meanwhile, R's father took his grandson's religious identity discrepancy into his own hands and managed to conduct a Hindu naming ceremony for the child when he was thirty days old, which angered J's family.

Continued work and visa matters meant that R's reunion with his wife and son was delayed for several years; poor telecommunication links further hampered the situation. J's family moved several times without telling R where they were going. R eventually was able to return home, but by then his marriage was apparently over. He still considered J to be his wife, though he was not sure where she was. R sadly reported that his son was now fifteen years old, and he had only seen him a few times. He also confided he had resigned himself to being a single man with no intention of finding another wife.

When asked about his faith, R said faith was still important to him, but he did not ascribe to a specific religion. He said he would advise others involved in an interfaith marriage not to convert their religion for the sake of the marriage. For this gentle and sincere man, the most difficult part of his marriage was the physical separation caused by his work, but that was compounded by religious interference and lack of family support.

Nearly all faith traditions have traditionally assumed that an interfaith marriage will only be successful if one partner converts. This was historically important when marriage was seen as a joining of communities or tribes with property and/or legal implications. A conversion was seen as eliminating, at least in theory, competing claims between beliefs and practices and ensuring a semblance of unified loyalties. "One faith will dominate" assumes that both partners will be able to practice their mutual religion together, that the religious upbringing of children is agreed upon, and that the couple has good potential for growing spiritually together.

In reality, "one faith will dominate" shares the shortcomings of the "no faith" and "separate faith" scenarios for the spiritual growth of interfaith couples, particularly if a coerced conversion is involved. Indeed, a forced conversion, even with the good intention of eliminating the religious differences of an interfaith couple, can have serious consequences for each spouse and the marriage. It effectively ignores or discounts the roots from which one spouse has grown and thereby stifles individual growth and mutual exploration. Several researchers indicate that this scenario often results in simmering resentment from the partner who converted. Richmond notes that most often it is the woman who converts, and often this is symptomatic of a power struggle within the relationship.[4] My own interviews with persons who converted for the sake of marriage revealed relationships, like R's, which were strained and often dysfunctional. I also interviewed several students from American College Madurai (South India) whose parents were from different faiths; their experience confirmed that insistence on conversion before marriage was not helpful and led to unhappy and unhealthy family dynamics.[5]

These same interviews indicated that conversion *after* marriage, based on personal decision rather than coercion, was not uncommon and indeed these marriages flourished when they provided openness and respect for the other. These reflect an understanding that, as in all aspects of life, growth involves change, and even in marriages in which both spouses start from similar faith perspectives, inevitably there are circumstances when one matures spiritually at a different rate than the other. In its most radical state, this change would be a religious conversion from one faith to another, though in reality smaller conversions are integral parts of spiritual growth.

---

4. See Richmond, *Blessed and Called*, 110, 127.
5. Interviews conducted at Madurai, S. India, on 21/22 February 2018.

Indeed, when conversion occurs on *faith* grounds, that is, when one partner (or both) decide that their personal faith development will be better addressed in another (shared) religion that is more in tune with their personal beliefs and practices, then many of the interfaith problems discussed earlier are eased. In situations where the birth religion of the partner(s) who converted is also respected, there is an extra bonus in the couple being able to appreciate and draw from a wider faith perspective and deeper roots. Such couples will still need to be mindful of and contend with the feeling issues that arise in times of conflict, feelings rooted in childhood faith backgrounds.

In a different scenario, when one spouse from a same-faith marriage decides to convert to another faith after marriage, the pair *becomes* an interfaith couple, even if this was not their original intention. Such a scenario requires a high level of personal trust and commitment to understanding the other for the marriage to succeed.

A Wider Harvest:
Maintaining and Supporting Both Faith Traditions

Perhaps the most challenging but potentially rewarding situation is one in which an interfaith couple agrees that they will maintain *both* their faith traditions, each supporting the other in their spiritual journey. Mary Helene Rosenbaum describes how her personal spiritual development has been nurtured by having a spouse who comes from a different faith tradition: "Marrying a Jew challenged my faith in a sense I had not foreseen. Whatever I did, I felt to a certain extent I was doing as a Catholic before a non-Catholic onlooker. This not only inspired me to be a better Catholic, it made me think about Catholic issues in a new way."[6]

The growth that comes from diligent and sustained listening, negotiating, and appreciating in such a hybrid marriage is often well worth the effort. Mutually supportive interfaith spouses frequently find they become *more rooted* and *committed* to their faith in such marriages, especially, though not exclusively, the partner who comes from the minority faith background.[7] They have intimate access to a wider perspective from which to explore personal faith issues. The resulting fuller appreciation of their

---

6. Rosenbaum and Rosenbaum, *Celebrating Our Differences,* 25.

7. Miller, *Being Both,* 186, 191.

own faith provides fertile ground for spiritual growth not just for themselves but for friends and extended family and further generations.

Raising Children: Pedigree or Hybrid?

The next challenge for interfaith couples is often deciding how to raise their children with regard to faith. The various traditional pedigree models assume that children follow the faith of their parents; indeed, as we've seen in cultures such as India's, one is born into a faith. In some religions, that birth faith is determined by the father's faith; in others, it is the mother's. For interfaith couples who have decided to each retain his/her own faith, the hybrid model of raising their children in both faith traditions is a still possibility. Susan Katz Miller's book, *Being Both,* provides convincing evidence that, when done well, this approach produces very positive results. Rather than being left to their own devices for understanding religious beliefs and practices, the children of both are endowed with a wealth of knowledge from which to make educated choices of the head and the heart.

I saw this model at work with the interfaith marriage support group meeting in a London church. Along with three married interfaith couples and two not-yet-married couples, four or five children were present, from babes in arms to a few older ones playing quietly just outside the circle of chairs. When I arrived, a lively conversation had begun on how to raise children to respect different faith traditions. One insisted it "doesn't happen by magic," and several others agreed that raising a child in a faith tradition must be intentional.

One couple described how they were teaching their young daughter to pray in two different ways, with full acceptance that she could choose which way she prefers. The mother explained that everyone is on a faith journey, and that interfaith marriage stretches one to identify and explore one's own faith beliefs. She and her husband were trying to pass this faith exploration journey on to their daughter so that she will have information and experience to eventually explore for herself. In all matters, including faith, they encourage their child to ask questions and be open to exploration. They say she already asks hard questions, such as what happens when one dies. When she asks, they are intentional about conferring with their spouse about what each feels/believes about the subject raised. "Give your child what you love about your religion," they advised. This conversation points to the potentially rich roots with which wise parents were seeking to supply their children, as well as ample impetus for interfaith couples to continue developing their own faith understandings and practices.

Gardening in a Larger Space: A Supporting Role for Faith Communities

Not only do interfaith couples need support from faith communities for their spiritual and communal journeys; the reverse is also true: faith communities can benefit from journeying with interfaith couples as they explore new understandings and perspectives on faith beliefs and practices. This communal task will require a different perspective from the faith groups who are accustomed to passing down traditions and dogma; instead, the task requires careful attention to the same hospitable practices which interfaith couples have had to learn: deep listening, respect, and reflection.

The interfaith couples' group met on the premises of a church whose stated intent was reaching out to the multifaith dimension of the community. I asked if the group had established—or knew of—groups that would help their children better understand their parents' different faiths. They explained that several of the children went to faith schools (though at such schools they would generally only learn one faith), but they didn't know of any multifaith schools. Most of them lived some distance from the church where the group met, so their meetings only happened about once a month and thus far did not include faith education for the children. They had heard of multifaith places of worship and family education elsewhere, but they did not know of any locally—though they wished such existed!

I asked the group what support they felt faith groups could/should offer to interfaith couples and families. They listed:

1. Welcome

2. Willingness to perform an interfaith wedding ceremony

3. Safe space, especially for young moms and children of interfaith couples

4. Support for the parents and family of interfaith couples

This aspirational list is instructive for faith communities.

Here is confirmation that individual faith congregations need to reexamine practices of welcome and how their hospitality will be perceived. Faith groups need to recognize that interfaith couples will often be very sensitive to whether they will be welcome—and some will be anxiously looking out for signs that they are *not* welcome. For one spouse, coming into a church might be like coming home; to the other, it will be like entering a foreign territory. Faith communities striving for hospitality need to ensure that both spouses feel they are welcome but not pressured to do or be or say anything.

At the same time, it is rather rare for interfaith couples to simply come through the door. The groundwork for such encounters more naturally emerges out of the congregation (or the faith leader) being recognized by the outside community as one interested in personal spiritual development, as well as interfaith relations. Groups for toddlers and young parents on the premises also provide potential signs of welcome. As with any meaningful outreach encounter, the establishment of a personal relationship most often precedes the willingness for an individual (or couple) to engage with the group.[8]

If an interfaith couple is brave enough to inquire about getting married in a faith venue, the clergy needs to be equipped to talk with the couple about what that endeavor would entail. There are several resources available for conducting weddings for interfaith couples.[9] It should be recognized as well that a nonreligious interfaith couple might choose a church as a wedding venue even though neither embraces Christianity; they might simply be bowing to cultural tradition which incorporates a nice venue. They might be subconsciously looking for welcome and accommodation, which could in time provide a link for further exploration of faith matters. Ultimately, each clergy person will be bound by the beliefs and practices of his/her religious group; the bottom line for Methodist ministers and churches is that our discipline *does* allow such ceremonies to take place. This single act of being willing to welcome and work with such a couple at this point in their lives is extremely important in setting the tone which might encourage them to decide that this congregation is indeed one in which they can remain and grow, and one with great potential for the spiritual growth of the host congregation as well.

The interfaith couples' group observation that their extended families need support highlights the fact that nearly all interfaith couples experience

8. It should also be noted that many Hindus, for instance, consider interfaith marriage an imperial instrument of coercion to convert.

9. See Macomb, *Joining Hands and Hearts*; Al-Yousuf and Birtwistle, "Marriage-Wedding FAQS."

some rejection from their families. The group members commented that acceptance of interfaith marriage amongst family members took time and required patience as parents and family were generally unprepared for the interfaith scenario, having been raised with the traditional understandings that interfaith marriage was taboo and would be detrimental to all. They felt their parents and families would also benefit from having a safe place to share with and learn from other interfaith families.

Each aspect of this hospitality on the part of the existing faith communities highlights the need to educate congregations on interfaith matters, even (or especially) those who are wary of interfaith encounters. Local congregations—house groups, study groups, and those gathered for worship—can be encouraged to think creatively about how they might enlarge their own hospitality. Leaders from other religious faiths can be invited to speak at services or with groups, though they will need to appreciate that this is not an appropriate venue for critiquing the beliefs of their host. Involvement with interfaith forums established across the UK can offer opportunities for meeting and learning from persons of other faiths, including visiting the worship venues for various religions. Members of congregations might want to visit other faith centers, as well as invite other faith groups to visit their church as well. Providing food is always a popular attraction, as long as dietary restrictions are considered.

Finally, there is a recognition that many, if not all, congregations already include persons who are in interfaith marriages or have family members who are. Often, these relationships have been kept quiet—or even secret—as the days of rejection and even humiliation for such are not that far in the past. Here is an opportunity to begin to build a support group for such persons, who might very well be eager to extend the support of the group to others. Here is an opportunity for mutual growth and interfaith exploration for all.

Summary

A successful marriage requires diligent work and adequate tools to allow the negotiation of differences, which produces creative growth. Interfaith couples may approach marriage with an even greater awareness of differences to negotiate, but their liminal experience can also produce an even more bountiful harvest: a deeper understanding of self and spouse and the faiths in which they were raised and from which they can draw. In turn, their understandings can help inform those with whom they come in contact: their families of origin, their offspring, and faith congregations.

As this research has highlighted the importance of faith development within marriage and of the lack of resources available for exploring faith issues within a contemporary interfaith marriage, part two of this book seeks to identify understandings from faith traditions that resonate with the present-day concept of marriage as a loving and faithful relationship of equals.

CHAPTER 7

Family, Faith, and Marriage

A Survey of Kodaikanal International School Alumni

FAITH AND INTERFAITH ISSUES are not only to be addressed by religious groups or within families themselves; schools, community centers, hospitals, hospices, and a variety of other community-based organizations can and do provide fertile opportunities for faith and interfaith understandings to grow and flourish. For twenty years (1978–98), my husband and I worked at an international school in South India that had made interfaith understanding one of its main functions long before it became fashionable or necessary for a well-rounded curriculum. I returned to the school some twenty years later to spend a few months writing and researching my interfaith marriage project further. It was then that I discovered just how important and effective that education had become for its alumni who now lived in communities across the globe.

Kodaikanal International School had begun in 1901 as a school for the children of Christian missionaries in South India. It was established in the town of Kodaikanal, a hill-station located 7000 feet above sea level, which had, in the previous century, attracted foreigners living and working in India who were more accustomed to cooler climates. They had flocked to the hills for respite, especially during the summer months when the temperatures soared on the plains. Kodai was especially popular with American Protestant missionaries who set up a residential school for their children, and what is known today as Kodai School was born.

As with many early missionary enterprises, the school was for many decades somewhat secluded from the rest of the town, but the school always had some intercultural elements just because it was set in South India. However secluded, during the first half of the school's existence, white missionary children were somehow interacting with the culture of multifaith India. In the 1970s, the school intentionally refocused on multiculturalism and rebranded itself as Kodaikanal International School (KIS). Its Christian (primarily Protestant) roots continued, but it deliberately welcomed and included students from a variety of faith traditions, even to the point of establishing a quota that at least half of the student population would be from other religions.

As with all such experiments in international living, there was much to learn, and the school didn't always get things right in terms of eliminating racism or colonialism or the urge to approach interfaith as an opportunity for conversion. Still, there was a will and intent to embrace education and residential living from an inclusive and mutually respectful attitude toward faith and faith traditions. Religious education classes were mandatory but began to include beliefs and practices of different faiths, and worship opportunities were made available for various religious groups. The International Baccalaureate academic program was adopted because of its multicultural curriculum and overall ethos of acceptance of diversity. Wearing one's national costumes on International Day celebrations and enjoying cultural programs and food from their various homes meant students (and staff) became aware of cultural differences and similarities. The staff of the residential dormitories received regular training in counseling and cross-cultural dynamics.

When I returned to Kodai in 2018 on a sabbatical, I was eager to see what had changed and what had remained the same. I anticipated conducting further research on interfaith marriages from an Indian context with groups down on the plain, but in the Kodai hills, I would just be writing. Soon after arriving in Kodai, though, I began to encounter various alumni from the school or the parents of KIS alumni who had married out. In our conversations, we began to wonder how the long-standing faith component of the Kodai School education had influenced KIS alumni in their marriages and spiritual development after they left the high misty hills. The conversations convinced me to conduct a survey of KIS alumni to establish baseline data on the faith practices of KIS alumni.

The "Family, Faith, and Marriage" survey was conducted on Survey-Monkey in March 2018 and received a record number of responses for a KIS survey: we heard from 270 alumni living in twenty-seven countries. The survey looked particularly at the faith(s) practiced in the childhood families of KIS alumni, their current faith practices, their incidence of marriage and marital satisfaction, and how they were raising their children with regard to faith. Responses came from those who had left the school in the 1940s up to the present, with about half reporting that they were involved in interfaith marriages.[1] While it would be misleading to claim that half of KIS alumni have married out, the data gleaned from the survey provides some important insights in the family, faith, and marriage trends of Kodai Kids and how the school's ethos shaped their ability to accommodate difference in the adult lives.

Family

The residential aspect of the school has meant it became home and family for virtually any student (or staff member) that attended, even if only for a few months, with the majority living in dormitories. From the earliest days, the school deliberately nurtured a family feel for the students and staff, as most were away from their own families for significant parts of each year. The somewhat isolated location also meant that almost anyone who went to Kodai to study came from somewhere else and thus found him/herself (willingly or otherwise) immersed in a new family, a new culture. Learning how to adapt to differences became an essential life skill. In previous chapters, we have spoken of how childhood experiences become formative for subconscious adult expectations in marriage and family life; the school's intent of developing attitudes of acceptance of difference become ingrained in the life of its students and staff. What most students don't fully appreciate during their time at Kodai is that the whole world doesn't function with the same attitudes, and that nearly all Kodai students will eventually indeed move away from that home and family.

As mentioned previously, the survey revealed that those from the Kodai alumni family who responded were residing in at least twenty-seven different countries and claiming twenty-three different nationalities. The

---

1. The initial results of the survey were somewhat skewed by a covering letter from the alumni office which suggested the survey was entirely about interfaith marriage, but after clarifications were made through social media, a wider variety of responses arrived.

majority lived in the USA (49 percent) or India (22 percent), with the rest spread across Canada, all parts of Asia, Australia and New Zealand, Europe, the Middle East, some parts of Africa, and even one in Costa Rica.[2] The most prevalent nationalities were Indian and American, but there were also Burmese, Bangladeshis, Bhutanese, Nepalese, Irish, Maltese, French, and a Peruvian. If part of the KIS education was about being a world citizen, able to adapt and survive in a variety of cultural situations, then the lesson appears to have been well learned.[3]

Fifty-eight percent of the respondents were female. While the school has long aimed for a fifty/fifty gender balance amongst its students, this slightly higher female response could be attributed to an assumption that females might be more attracted to the Family, Faith, and Marriage topic— or that KIS indeed has encouraged females to use their voices.

Faith

In today's world, international schools are not the only learning institutions that have students and staff from diverse ethnic backgrounds. Indeed, schools around the world have become more diverse, especially those in urban or cosmopolitan areas. Kodai School's decision in the mid-1970s to become more intentionally international and intercultural was closely linked with its determination to remain a faith school. It continued to understand itself as a Christian school as well. The dichotomy of being a Christian International School made perfect sense to some and was viewed as nonsense by others, but a core principle was the belief that faith is essential for well-being and developing maturity. Many school curricula across the world today have also become more intentionally inclusive of various faith traditions, though often the intent seems to be nurturing an appreciation of diversity rather than nurturing faith.

2. Countries of residence included: USA, India, Canada, S. Korea, China, Japan, Singapore, Sri Lanka, Malaysia, Australia, New Zealand, the UK, Luxembourg, Germany, Switzerland, Sweden, Cyprus, Albania, Spain, Tanzania, Kenya, Israel, Kuwait, UAE, Saudi Arabia, and Costa Rica.

3. It is interesting to note that 52 percent of those responding indicated they were born in India, but 49 percent of the respondents were living in the USA. Rather than only indicating a brain drain from East to West, the data rather reveals the high number of KIS students (especially before 2000) who were US citizens born to parents living and working in India. The number of those born in India with Indian nationality who were living in the USA remained relatively low at 28 percent.

The survey showed how that change from being a Christian Protestant-only institution, to being a multifaith institution manifested itself in its former students' identification of the faith of their birth families. The oldest alumni respondents all came from Christian Protestant families, but only 30 percent of alumni leaving KIS after 1990 reported coming from Christian Protestant homes. Overall, about half of those doing the survey came from Christian Protestant homes, which agrees broadly with the school's admission statistics over the past several decades.

Another question asked what religion they identified with as an adult. The responses received included (in order of popularity): Christian Protestant, None, Hindu, Christian Catholic, atheist, Muslim, Buddhist, Zoroastrian, Jewish, Jain, Christian Orthodox, Unitarian Universalist, agnostic, Ismaili, Quaker, and a variety of hybrids. The survey data revealed that about 35–40 percent of KIS alumni changed their adult faith identification from that of their childhood family, a statistic which is consistent with current norms in the USA.[4] Those who changed their faith had primarily been brought up in the Christian Protestant, Hindu, and Zoroastrian traditions. The largest *increase* in adult faith identification came from those currently declaring themselves Nones, agnostics, or atheists; their numbers peaked with KIS alumni in the 1990s and are broadly comparable to worldwide trends.

Roman Catholic students were the first non-Protestants to join the school in the 1960s, followed in the 1970s by Hindus, and in the 1980s by an influx of Zoroastrians. Those born into Catholic homes were most consistent in retaining their childhood faith identity, along with those from Muslim, Jain, Jewish, and Christian Orthodox groups who also arrived later at KIS. These consistency trends coincide with some research claiming that those from minority religions often retain their identities in the midst of multifaith scenarios, while the majority religions often see decreases from their adherents in multifaith scenarios. This latter theory is confirmed by the statistics showing that percentages of those alumni currently identifying as Christian Protestant (majority faith of the school population) and Hindu (majority faith of India) as adults decreased by about one-third from the number who indicated those as their family faiths. A notable anomaly in the survey results concerns adherents to Buddhism which, while still low

4. Riley (reporting on a Faith Matters survey done for *Amazing Grace*), *'Til Faith Do Us Part*, 58.

in number, more than doubled in those who currently considered themselves Buddhists but grew up in another faith tradition.

Marriage

It is one thing to assemble a diverse faith population; it is another to provide them with tools to co-exist peaceably. I wondered how KIS's emphasis on learning to live with diversity was reflected in the marital life of its alumni.

Two-thirds of those responding to the survey declared themselves currently married, with another 12 percent separated, divorced, or widowed. About one in five had never married (partly because many of the respondents are still in their twenties and thirties and so had not yet married). KIS alumni, with their lived experience of close contact with those of other faiths, appear to have approached the potential marriage market with an enlarged sense of what faith they could live with in a marriage partner. Indeed, 52 percent of the married respondents reported having a spouse from another faith, though as noted above, this survey sample does not necessarily represent the whole of the school's alumni. The largest number of those marrying out in this survey came from the Christian Protestant tradition (43 percent), which was not too unusual as this group comprises the largest percentage of KIS's alumni population. Those from Catholic families had the highest percentage of marrying out, with 88 percent, while the Nones were at 81 percent.

More importantly, 92 percent of all married respondents reported satisfaction in their marriage; those in interfaith marriages reported an 85 percent satisfaction rate. Both these are very high results compared with the 80 percent satisfaction rate cited for the USA.[5] This appears to confirm that KIS students indeed learned some important skills for living with others in close relationships.

As noted in previous chapters, the large increase in the numbers of interfaith marriages across the world has not always met with a corresponding level of support for those couples and families, and this was also the case for several KIS alumni who revealed that marrying out had led to conflicts with parents and families. Happily, in most cases, those from KIS had been spared the outright rejection experienced by interfaith couples elsewhere. For example, the survey showed a high acceptance of interfaith marriages

5. Riley (reporting on a Faith Matters survey done for *Amazing Grace*), '*Til Faith Do Us Part*, 124.

by Christian Protestant families, a statistic that is somewhat surprising as this faith has a reputation for exclusivity. On the other hand, nearly all KIS Muslims involved in interfaith marriage had experienced rejection by their families.

Marital Dissatisfaction

While the KIS alumni survey showed a high percentage of marital satisfaction, the responses of those who were somewhat or very dissatisfied deserve a closer look. *Those most dissatisfied with their marriages were Nones or atheists involved in interfaith marriages,* almost twice the average of the general respondents. Indeed, more than half of the Nones reported being divorced or separated, compared with 7 percent of the overall KIS alumni. As noted earlier, many involved in interfaith marriages decide it is easier to be None than to negotiate religious differences; indeed, a 2018 Pew Study lists interfaith marriage as one of the reasons given by Christians for becoming Nones, though it is not cited as a major contributor.[6] The fact that a high percentage of Nones are dissatisfied with their marriages might suggest a correlation between marital satisfaction and the development of spirituality.

Marital dissatisfaction was also very high for those who experienced at least some rejection from their families when they chose to marry someone from another faith (93 percent, compared with 19 percent of general KIS respondents). In many cases, this familial rejection would have been on religious grounds, thus providing a reason for the one facing rejection to in turn reject his/her birth religion. Going further, a higher percentage of those who were dissatisfied with their interfaith marriage also reported that they had no support for their marriage, either from family, friends, or a faith tradition (35 percent, compared with 23 percent of the general responses). While marital dissatisfaction has many causes, this exploration with KIS alumni illustrates that, like forced conversion, faith traditions which reject interfaith marriage on the basis of exclusivist religious claims can have the unintended effect of producing dysfunctional marriages—to which the initial detractors may unhelpfully point out that it was never going to work anyway. The question arises: How is one's faith—or marriage—to develop when the support structures have been removed?

6. Pew Research Center, "Being Christian in Western Europe," 87.

Generational Patterns

This survey also provided preliminary data for tracing generational trends in interfaith marriage. For instance, in this survey, three out of four respondents reported that their parents had been in same-faith marriages and about half of those with same-faith parents had themselves married within their faith tradition. On the other hand, well over half (59 percent) of those who grew up with interfaith parents had married spouses from other faiths. With some data emerging for yet a third generation of marriage statistics, 13 percent of both same-faith and interfaith couples reported that at least one of their children had married out.

Cohabitation and Same-Sex Marriage

While this survey's title spoke of Family, Faith, and *Marriage*, cohabitation was noted as a growing trend amongst KIS alumni, as it is seen as a contemporary alternative to married life in many societies across the world. Cohabitating KIS alumni reported living in and coming from a variety of localities and faith backgrounds. Seventy percent of their partners had come from different faith backgrounds than their own. As cohabitation is a relatively new phenomenon, it has a very low approval rating in virtually all faith traditions, and accordingly, these persons reported that they had a very low rate (33 percent) of support for their personal faith development.[7]

Final Observations

Overall, this survey suggested that KIS's emphasis on providing both a multicultural/multifaith environment, along with a deliberate emphasis on developing positive relationships in the midst of diversity, had prepared its students well for satisfactory marital situations, including interfaith marriage. The statistics also revealed a generally high engagement with personal faith development amongst the school's alumni, though there were some situations in which they struggled to find faith support. Several of those responding to the survey commented on the perceived differences between religion, faith, and spirituality, with the latter often preferred as a

---

7. The prevalence of same-sex marriage and partnerships is also a global trend. With the low percentage in this survey declaring themselves involved in same-sex relationships, their overall data was included in the general analyses of marriage and faith data.

term allowing for more personal choice in faith development, a trend we've seen in contemporary society in general. While the school has respected this choice of spirituality in personal development, the contemporary tendency to set the *personal* in opposition to the *corporate* nature of religion poses some conflict with the KIS ethos of communal support for faith development. Indeed, an insistence on the personal often effectively removes the support that is available through the faith community. The school's active hiking program in the hills of South India was a practical enforcer of McLennan's analogy of mountain-climbing to describe the journey of spiritual development. KIS alumni would know that climbing the mountain is considerably easier with an experienced guide, and the journey is much more enjoyable in the company of others.

Along with sifting through the data presented by this survey, I was privileged to conduct several interviews with individual respondents, both in person and through email. Several of these mentioned marital and/or faith situations encountered after they left Kodai and in which they have struggled, often on their own. The reality of a residential (boarding) school situation is that once one leaves the front gate, one has often lost one's effective support network and even direct connection with that which has built and informed one's value system. Unlike leaving one's family as a young adult, it is much harder to return home on a regular basis to a boarding school. More than one interviewee commented that once s/he left KIS, s/he had to learn that everyone s/he met could not be trusted. While this is a sad commentary on our contemporary world, it also affirms the importance of setting aspirational models of trust and respect in the formative years. These foundations can inform lifelong attitudes of acceptance and accommodation of differences, if only in the recognition that such practices are indeed possible.

PART TWO

Introduction
Theologies of Marriage

MARRIAGE IS AN INTIMATE and crucial working space for human couples committed to living with and loving each other over an extended period. Such committed relationships can also provide opportunities for couples to grow spiritually. An interfaith marriage can provide incentives for each to dig deeper into the faith traditions they and their partner have grown up in, an opportunity to examine religious roots and explore embedded faith scripts. Interfaith marriage partners have an ongoing daily opportunity to develop insights which can help reconcile religious differences, as well as add new perspectives to faith. Understanding and accepting each other's religious background in an interfaith marriage becomes a valuable tool for renegotiating one's own beliefs and traditions, and an opportunity to explore the benefits and liabilities, strengths and weaknesses, insights and blind spots of each tradition. Exploring faith traditions and practices together can reveal new resources for mutual thriving and personal growth. "We not only need to know the others; we also need the others to know ourselves."[1]

The following chapters will explore the theological basis of marriage in each of seven separate religious traditions: the Jewish, Christian, Islamic, Hindu, Buddhist, Zoroastrian, and Bahá'í faiths. These explorations are based on the scriptures of each faith tradition, fully recognizing that traditions continue to evolve and respond to contemporary cultural

---

1. Eck, former moderator of the World Council of Churches Sub-unit on Dialogue, cited in Ariarajah, *Not without My Neighbour*, 48.

surroundings.[2] Our explorations will be based on primary texts rather than historical developments, seeking foundational theological truths concerning marriage and spiritual development, such as: How and why were humans created? What is the purpose of life for men and women, husbands and wives? Does marriage help or hinder each to fulfill his/her creative purposes?

We will seek to tease out from the ancient texts insights that address contemporary understandings of marriage, such as whether marriage can be seen as more than an institution to regulate procreation: Can marriage be regarded as a vehicle for personal maturity and spiritual development? Do these marriage traditions offer possibilities for social stability other than, or through, the regulation of sexual activity? How do the various faith traditions inform contemporary understandings of equality, both in terms of gender and respect for other faith traditions?

Some will counter that virtually all faith traditions are based on patriarchal models, so no religion can be said to uphold gender equality. Ariarajah points out, "Most traditions pushed women back into a subordinate position, fixed their roles in the family and society, barred them from interpreting scriptures and denied them the kind of leadership that would bring about real change."[3] Digging deeper into the scripture texts can also remind us that an original purpose of patriarchy was to empower a few for the responsibility of providing protection for the whole. We also recognize that, while virtually all the founders of the world's major religions made significant efforts to *enhance* the place of women in their societies, various traditions and interpretations of scriptures gradually reversed these advances in favor of male domination.

Virtually all religions have also at some point affirmed the validity of other faith traditions. Though most religious traditions are still reluctant to encourage the literal "embrace of the other" that comes through interfaith marriage,[4] this exploration of multiple faith traditions is done in a spirit of

---

2. Ariarajah notes: " . . . [I]t is important to recognize not only the plurality of religions but also the plurality *within* religions . . . When someone has problems with Christianity, Islam or Hinduism, it is important to sort out what we are talking about. Consciousness of this can bring greater clarity amidst the confusions that prevail" (*Not without My Neighbour,* 22 [italics original]).

3. Ariarajah, *Not without My Neighbour,* 64.

4. As Romain has reflected: "'Love your neighbour as yourself' . . . [t]hat sort of [interfaith marital] love was never envisaged in the sacred texts" (*Till Faith Us Do Part,* 19).

respect and patient prodding toward a common goal of spiritual maturity and mutual understanding.

CHAPTER 8

Marriage in Judaism

BY JONATHAN ROMAIN

THE PRIMARY SOURCE FOR Judaism is the Hebrew Bible, also known as the Old Testament. However, unlike the New Testament, which covers the lifetime of Jesus and a few decades after his death, or the Qur'an, which centers on the prophet Muhammad, the Hebrew Bible spans several centuries. It means that even within that primary text, on the one hand the key themes of marriage and relationships are established, but on the other hand there are considerable developments over the period it covers. There have also been many shifts in perspective and regulations in Jewish life since then.

This is evident in the first-ever couple, Adam and Eve, whether they be seen as historical figures or a template for humans in general (it is significant that in Hebrew, Adam means "man" and Eve means "life"). For their union, no ceremony is involved, but as Genesis 4:1 puts it, "And the man knew Eve his wife," with the verb that is used in the Hebrew original indicating physical intimacy, indicating that marriage and sex were inextricably linked. This can be taken in two senses. First, that having a sexual relationship is one of the privileges of marriage and is an act reserved for one's partner. Second, that a sexual relationship between two adults meant they were married and should be seen by the rest of society as a unit. Both aspects have influenced Judaism throughout the ages. In the case of the former, it meant that sexual union was to be reserved for one person only, both as a contract to be observed and as a bond that enhanced the relationship. In the case of the latter, it meant that, in Jewish law, the child of two adults who were free to have sex with each other was not considered illegitimate. A child was only considered a bastard if it was the product of a forbidden sexual relationship, such as incest or adultery.

What is entirely absent from the initial chapters of the Bible is the mention of personal feelings between couples. This does not mean feelings were absent, but rather that the Bible typically concentrates in any given episode on what it considers the key theme and tends to leave out details that are not strictly relevant. Unlike a novelist, who will often give a description of the natural setting in which the hero or heroine is walking, or of the weather conditions warming or chilling them, the Bible is a guide to life and wants to focus on the main action.

In Adam and Eve's case, marriage is about procreation, both to continue their existence into another generation and to help tame the hard world in which they find themselves. Marriage is pragmatic, a means of managing the present and planning the future. We must assume the same of the next two couples we encounter, the first of which is Noah and his wife. It is very noticeable that although we know the names of their three sons—Shem, Ham and Japheth—we never discover her name. She obviously had one, and it would not have been too much trouble to relay it to us, but the Bible wants to move on with the story and what happens next. Of course, it could also be indicative of the less important and much limited role that a wife had in the then-patriarchal society. She had produced children and that was all that mattered. Her own personality and needs were very secondary.

This seems to be a similar pattern in the case of the founding father of Judaism, Abraham. We do hear a lot about Sarah but little about their relationship. The only time that feelings are involved is when she demands the expulsion of her handmaid, Hagar, initially because of her the rivalry between them (Gen 16:4–6) and later because she feared for the future of her son Isaac (Gen 21:9–10). Sarah does feature again when her beauty leads a local ruler to attempt to take her for himself, but God intervenes to restore her to Abraham, and it is made clear that she is his property (Gen 12:11–19). Marriage therefore meant both boundaries and, in those days, possession. Sarah certainly seems to have had no say in the two momentous events in Abraham's life: neither the decision to uproot themselves from Ur of the Chaldees to journey to the land of Israel, nor the intention to sacrifice Isaac—although some rabbinic commentators suggest that the reason Abraham "rose early in the morning" (Gen 22:3) was to avoid Sarah discovering his plan and intervening to thwart it.

It is only in the next generation that the idea of love is mentioned, when Rebecca is chosen as a wife for Isaac and we are told that he "took Rebecca [i. e., had sex with her], and she became his wife, and he loved her" (Gen 24:67). Once again, marriage is signaled by consummation, but for the first time we hear of the development of a personal relationship. Rabbinic commentators over the ages have made great play of the order of the words: marriage came first and love came second. It implies, they say, that marriage is primarily a partnership to provide mutual support—he hunts for food, she breeds children—but as a result of this, an emotional bond can emerge. Unlike the contemporary sequence of falling in love and then marrying a person, in Genesis we have the reverse: marriage comes first and then love will grow after getting to know each other and working together. This is still the justification behind arranged marriages today, both amongst the ultra-Orthodox Jews (though not other Jews) and in some groups within other faiths.

What is so intriguing about the Isaac-Rebecca relationship is that although this love was a very positive aspect, ultimately, they proved to be a couple who lacked compatibility. They each favored a different child—he favored Esau, while she preferred Jacob—which is not a sin in itself but hints that they may have found more satisfaction in their children than in each other. This then leads to a betrayal of marital trust when Rebecca actually conspires with Jacob against her husband. They cheat the blind Isaac into thinking that Jacob is Esau and that Jacob should receive the birthright he covets but which rightfully belongs to Esau. It is a relationship that warns that love is not enough by itself, but needs to be accompanied by communication, respect, and trust.

Jacob, by contrast, does find perfect harmony in the form of Rachel as his wife, and their romance can almost be seen as the biblical Romeo and Juliet: passionate love with major complications. The first is that her father, Laban, refuses to let them marry unless Jacob earns her by working for him for seven years. Then he tricks Jacob into marrying her older sister, Leah—on the cultural grounds that the older sister should marry before the younger—and only agrees to Jacob marrying his true love the following week if he works another seven years for her (Gen 29:18–28), which he duly did. The depth of their relationship is evident in the name he gives their second child when she dies after giving birth to him: Benjamin, which means in Hebrew, "son of my right hand."

However, the Jacob story is also problematic in that it indicates that the Bible permitted polygamy, as happened in numerous other cases, too. In later times, the rabbis came to regard monogamy as preferable, as is the norm today, but they felt unable to condemn the Bible outright. Instead, they held that customs that were appropriate in those days were no longer so in subsequent periods. As with the institution of slavery or animal sacrifices, along with the patriarchal system in family life and the priestly role in religious life, polygamy ranks as one of several aspects of the Bible that are deemed to have passed their sell-by date.

If the book of Genesis provides the two central elements of marriage—partnership and relationship—one must wait for a much later biblical text for another feature: sexual attraction. The Song of Songs (sometimes referred to as the Song of Solomon) is a no-holds-barred erotic text. Interestingly, it is not a one-sided account, but from the perspective of both the man and the woman. Thus she declares: "My beloved is to me as a bag of myrrh that lies between my breasts . . . Behold you are handsome, my beloved, very attractive and our bed is luscious" (Song 1:13, 16) His response includes: "Your lips are like a thread of scarlet, and your mouth is inviting . . . Your two breasts are like two fawns that are twins of a gazelle" (Song 4:3, 5).

In fact, when the rabbis came to canonize the Bible, there were many who argued that the Song of Songs was far too sexually explicit for a holy text and should be omitted. It was only after one of the leading figures of the time, Rabbi Akiva, intervened and claimed that it was an allegory of the love between God and Israel, not a description of human lust, that it was included.

There is no doubt that both in biblical texts and modern Judaism marriage is seen as a powerful and beneficial institution. However, there is also the awareness that it can have flaws, be it with matches that were unsuitable or unions that go wrong. The Hebrew Bible, therefore, has no objection to couples admitting this and gaining a divorce. As the old Jewish adage puts it: "Better an end with pain, than pain without end." The book of Deuteronomy lays out the procedure for divorce in detail, and although it is a process that can only be initiated by the man, it is not seen as something shameful (Deut 24:1). Moreover, both ex-partners are then free to remarry someone else. It demonstrates that, unlike the approach adopted in some parts of the Christian church, marriage was taken as a free-will act and never became a sacrament before God[1]; just as it could be undertaken freely, so it could be ended freely. Of course, the hope was always that the first marriage would be successful and last for a lifetime, but it could be undone if that proved not to be the case.

Despite the Hebrew Bible's promotion of marriage, it is well aware of human faults and frailties. It is perhaps for that reason that "You shall not commit adultery" is included as one of the Ten Commandments (Exod 20:13). After all, there is no point banning something that nobody does in the first place. The command is made explicit precisely because of the temptation to stray from the marital bed. In this respect, the Bible does not shy away from representing not only what should happen, but what actually takes place. A whole catalogue of sexual misdemeanors is to be found in the biblical books: adultery, rape, sodomy, incest, prostitution, and homosexuality (though the latter is seen in a very different light nowadays). These cases are all individual acts, but they take their most dramatic form in the book of Hosea where the prophet is commanded to marry a prostitute as an image representing the people of Israel's infidelity to God (Hosea 1:2; 3:1). The fact that so many other prophets also use the same image indicates not only the people's religious backsliding, but that the prevalence of prostitution made it a powerful and instantly recognizable comparison.

Another marital issue that the Hebrew Bible considers worth mentioning is marrying out of the faith. The issue was not racial prejudice but religious purity. That is why Abraham instructed his servant Eliezer to find a suitable wife for Isaac from far away and not from "the daughters of the Canaanites amongst whom I dwell" (Gen 24:3). The latter would be attached to the local gods and might influence Isaac to worship them likewise. Someone from out of the area would not expect her local god to travel with her, and so she would become attached to Isaac's faith. She would also lack any local support for her former faith, be it fellow-worshipers or sacred tree. This was especially important for Abraham, given that he had just established an entirely new faith, knew it lacked strong roots, and was keen to ensure it continued after his death. However, it became a theme throughout Israelite history, with constant exhortations, from Moses to the later prophets, not to be beguiled into adopting local pagan practices and beliefs through intermarriage. Even before they had entered the promised land, the Israelites were commanded not to intermarry with the inhabitants

---

1. Ed. note: marriage is only considered a sacrament in some parts of Christianity, particularly Roman Catholicism.

for that reason. Seven nationalities were specified as taboo: the Hittites, Girgashites, Amorites, Canaanites, Perizzites, Hivites, and Jebusites (Deut 7:1–3).

This prohibition had dramatic reinforcement in an episode during the Israelites' forty years of wandering in the wilderness. The fear of pagan contamination is recorded in the book of Numbers when "Israel abode in Shittim and the people began to develop intimate relationships with the daughters of Moab. The latter enticed the people to the sacrifices of their gods, and the people did eat and bowed down to their gods" (Num 25:1–2). God's reaction is swift and deadly, declaring that the Israelite men who had engaged in idolatry should face the death penalty. It was then that a particularly zealous individual, Pinchas, took matters into his own hands, although coming from within the hierarchy, being the grandson of Aaron the high priest. Pinchas heard of an Israelite man having sex with a Midianite woman, entered their tent and thrust them both through with a spear (Num 25:6–8). Moreover, he was then praised for this act and rewarded by being given God's covenant of peace. It is noticeable, though, that he does not feature in the future leadership of the Israelites during the time of Moses, perhaps because though zealotry may have its merits, it is not the best qualification for decision-making.

There were, however, many cases of biblical figures marrying non-Jews other than from the seven nations, including those very attached to other faiths. They include Joseph marrying an Egyptian priest's daughter and Moses marrying a Midianite priest's daughter. But in the culture of the era, it was assumed the woman simply adopted the husband's faith, and that any children followed the faith of their father. An active process of conversion itself is not mentioned in the Hebrew Bible, although later tradition looked back at the book of Ruth as providing a template. Her ringing declaration that "your people shall be my people and your God shall be my God" (Ruth 1:16) was seen as a formal declaration of conversion and a demonstration that personal sincerity was an essential ingredient. However, even in that verse, it is clear she was joining the community as much as the faith itself.

What is also remarkable about the Ruth episode is that she becomes the great grandmother of David, who became seen as the idealized king and from whose line the messiah would emerge one day. Without an Israelite man marrying the Moabite Ruth—who only converted after his death—a key aspect of both Jewish history and Jewish theology would not have happened! Taken side by side with the opposition to intermarriage voiced earlier, this highlights both the advantages and disadvantages of intermarriage. On the one hand it can bring added members to the community—which is especially important in a small community concerned about its long-term sustainability—as well as lead to fresh thinking and new opportunities. On the other hand it can lead to religious dilution for the individual concerned and mean the loss of his or her line and future generations. Much depends on whether the Jewish person is marrying out and effectively abandoning the faith (be it intentional or not), or if the non-Jewish person is marrying in and aligning themselves with the Jewish way of life. The former can lead to a halving of numbers, the latter to a doubling of numbers. Crucial too, certainly in today's context, is whether the surrounding family and community is welcoming or hostile. This can determine whether the non-Jewish partner feels at home in Jewish life or resentful of it.

Two factors at the end of the biblical period changed the earlier relaxed attitude to conversion and intermarriage to a more negative, if not hostile, one. First, the exile to Babylon and elsewhere meant that Jewish life was no longer the dominant faith of the land and so anyone becoming Jewish had to consciously opt into a minority religion rather than just integrate into the surrounding culture. In fact, it is in the book of Esther, which is situated in Shushan in Persia, that the people are no longer referred to as Hebrew or Israelites but, for the first time, as Jews (Esther 3:4, 6). They were no longer a resident people, but a faith group. Second, as a result of Ezra's reforms (Ezra 10:3), the definition of Jewish status switched from being determined by whether one had a Jewish father to whether one had a Jewish mother. It effectively extended the ban on intermarriage from the daughters of the seven nations specified above—which, in reality, had long disappeared—to a ban on marriage with any non-Jewish woman unless she formally converted to Judaism, otherwise one's children would not be Jewish. It was based on the same fear as in earlier periods that intermarriage would threaten the Jewish person's faith and the continuity of their line.

From the time of Abraham at the beginning of the Hebrew Bible to Ezra at its end (in the Jewish order of the books), there was a deeply ingrained awareness of how fragile the survival of Judaism was and how carefully it needed to be guarded. There were some later attempts at an active missionary campaign, such as the forcible conversion of the Idumeans by Hyrcanus I about 120 BCE, though that was largely motivated by political factors to secure the kingdom. On a more religious level were subsequent efforts by the Pharisees, who were described as crossing "sea and land to make a single proselyte" (Matt 23:15), but these were sporadic activities. Moreover, once Constantine converted to Christianity, there were a series of laws forbidding attempts to convert others to Judaism. Instead, holding onto existing Jews through marriage and family were seen as the main ways of preserving the faith and nurturing the next generation into it.

Attitudes have changed in some Jewish groups who today are more willing to accommodate intermarriage, but for many centuries after the Bible it was seen as a threat to the faith and a curse that Jewish parents wanted to avoid. This also explains how being Jewish is often more a matter of family identity than of individual spirituality. For many Jews, a sense of belonging supersedes issues of faith. Similarly, what happens in the home is regarded as an equally important conduit for the faith as what goes on in the synagogue. A home that is religiously divided is seen as, at best, a challenge to the Jewish future and, at worst, totally incompatible with it. If the non-Jewish person converts, however, then that is no longer counted as an intermarriage and they are considered as fully Jewish as one who is born a Jew. It is no surprise, therefore, that one of the popular definitions of a Jew is a person who has Jewish grandchildren. It concentrates much more on their ability to perpetuate the faith than on their relationship with God. The two are not mutually exclusive, but the emphasis is telling.

CHAPTER 9

Human Purpose, Spiritual Maturity, and Marriage in Christian Scripture

To EXPLORE A CHRISTIAN theology of marriage, we will search for biblical understandings of how and why humans were created, how they are to achieve spiritual maturity, and whether marriage promotes spiritual growth. Much early Christian theology and practice grew out of Jewish faith traditions found in the Hebrew Bible (also known as the Old Testament in many Christian circles). Christian understandings of marriage developed further with the teachings of Jesus Christ and the theological insights of St. Paul which are found in the New Testament.

Christians understand the purpose of human life to be summed up in the teaching of Jesus: "Love the Lord your God with all your soul and mind and strength . . . and your neighbor as yourself."[1] This teaching had deep roots in the Jewish tradition known as the Law and the Prophets. The Law was summed up in the Ten Commandments, which included honoring one's parents and respecting and protecting the dignity of others by refraining from murdering, stealing, or lying. The Hebrew prophets expanded these acts and attitudes to explicitly include loving and caring for others: "Do justice, love kindness (or mercy), and walk humbly with God" (Micah 6:8).

In the New Testament Gospels of Matthew, Mark, and Luke, Jesus expanded the concept of neighbor through his words and actions to include virtually all others within and outside one's community, even those

---

1. Matt 22:37; Mark 12:30; Luke 10:27—all references from NRSV.

traditionally and intentionally excluded, such as the hated Samaritans. Since the New Testament writers recognized Jesus as both human and divine, his words and actions carried clues as to how humans were to behave. In John's Gospel, Jesus says: "Love each other as I have loved you" (15:12), and the examples given show that one's neighbor is to be loved in the context of washing the other's feet, caring, feeding, forgiving, and even dying for the other. As one's spouse could be included in this portrayal of neighbor, marriage comes firmly within the scope of fulfilling one's human purpose: to love God and others.

Jesus' teaching about love and respect for the other, growing out of Jewish traditions, also came at a time when Greco-Roman philosophy had significantly relaxed attitudes toward sex and marriage practice.[2] One of Jesus' significant contributions was to reinterpret many Jewish concepts and traditions of his day, including those of marriage and gender roles. That pattern of reinterpretation continues to this day within Christian circles. In today's Christianity, there are conservative and progressive views on marriage and gender roles, each basing their theology on the biblical texts. In line with our aim to identify perspectives within each religion that will support marriages in contemporary society, we will seek principles of egalitarian gender roles from the Christian Scriptures.

Creation of Humanity

The book of Genesis presents two versions of how and why God created humans, each coming from a slightly different theological perspective. The version in the first chapter starts with the familiar "In the beginning . . . " and outlines a seven-day account of God establishing and ordering the world out of a chaotic void. Essential to this account is the principle that God deems this creation to be "good." This first account also presents the creation of humans as God's crowning achievement, one which God rated "very good" (Gen 1:31). It is especially noteworthy that humans were created "in God's image" and that they were created as "male and female" (Gen 1:27), equal beings with equal goodness and potential.

The second creation account follows immediately in Genesis 2 with God creating a human, *'Adam*, from the soil of the earth—the word *'Adam* originally comes from a word meaning "ground"—and *'Adam* comes to life as God's breath/spirit is breathed into his nostrils. After several attempts to

2. Johnson and Jordan, "Christianity," 78.

produce a suitable companion for the lone human, God creates a woman from 'Adam's rib while he is sleeping, crucially indicating that she is created from the same substance as he, and thus fundamentally equal in substance. A few chapters later (Gen 5:2), both the man and the woman are known collectively as 'Adam (now meaning "humankind"), which further establishes the two as created of the same matter.

These first two chapters of Genesis usually form the basis of Judeo-Christian understandings of marriage, though in reality there is no actual reference to marriage here, only a reference to the couple being blessed by God and then told to "be fruitful and multiply" (Gen 1:28).[3] Still, this passage has been assumed to agree with nearly all primitive understandings of marriage that the primary purpose of a man and woman joining in a committed relationship was procreation.

The second story, however, relates their coming together—their marriage—in terms not confined to procreation: "Therefore a man leaves his father and his mother and clings to his wife, and they become one flesh" (Gen 2:24). This passage lays out an understanding of marriage as a moving beyond one's childhood (leaving home) by taking on a spouse, a companion with whom one becomes one flesh. While the sexual dynamic is implied in the expression "one flesh," the subsequent garden of Eden story initially depicts the couple delighting in each other's companionship rather than simply focusing on procreation. This understanding is foundational for a contemporary Judeo-Christian understanding of marriage.

The garden of Eden story also tells of the fall of Adam and Eve, in which they are punished for disobedience, an account which many interpret as assigning blame to the woman for bringing evil into the world. In the actual biblical account, the blame and repercussions are shared by both: the woman is promised pain in childbirth and subjection to her husband, while the man is assigned the hard task of laboring to provide food. This assignment of gender roles aligned with reproductive functions resembles patterns found in virtually all faith traditions and includes a woman's subjection to her husband as part of a patriarchal understanding of marriage. It is worth noting, though, that both the male and the female are then banished from the garden. While the specific punishments are often cited as God-given roles for wife/husband, these are not presented as God's original intent for the pair but a consequence of *human* disobedience and sin.

---

3. Greenberg, "Marriage in the Jewish Tradition," 429.

Marriage Relations in the Hebrew Bible

Beginning with the book of Genesis, the Hebrew Bible is filled with stories of husbands and wives illustrating a huge gamut of marital relations: monogamous, polygamous, endogamous (spouses who are close relatives), and exogamous (spouses from outside the tribe, including foreigners). Producing offspring is regarded as an important aspect of marriage, evident in the several accounts of the plight of barren women. Stories such as that of Abraham and Sarah (who remained with each other through many infertile decades; Gen 12–20) and, indeed, Abraham and Hagar (whom Abraham sent away after they had had a child together; Gen 17), confirm however that procreation is not the sole determiner of the quality of marriage relationships.

The polygamous assumptions of the Jewish kings (beginning, but not ending, with Saul, David, and Solomon) indicate that marriage was also seen in terms of gaining political advantage with one's neighbors and/or competitors. Nearly all these stories are told from an understanding that the survival and flourishing of the family (and societal) unit depended on the male's ability to provide and protect and the woman's complementary role as wife and mother, nurturing the family. In the process of developing a strong patriarchal system which protected the family, however, the needs of women who fell outside the parameters of normal marital relations were severely neglected. A woman's worth in society was based on her fertility and connection with a male, which meant a woman whose marital ties had been severed for whatever reasons had very little status or means for survival on her own. The much-beloved story of the widow Ruth and her also-widowed mother-in-law, Naomi, reveals the strongly patriarchal hierarchy which renders the two women virtually destitute until Ruth is married by Naomi's kinsman, Boaz.[4] Even the self-assured businesswoman and entrepreneur now known as the Proverbs 31 woman is still named first as a "capable *wife*," and as such, her primary role is assumed to be caring for her husband and his needs.

Sexuality is an important topic in the Hebrew Scriptures, though a wide variety of approaches are present. On one hand the Hebrew Scriptures include the Song of Songs (also known as the Song of Solomon), with

---

4. This story, from the book of Ruth, is a prime example of an ancient interfaith marriage which met with some degree of acceptance, especially in light of Ruth being named as one of only four women listed in Matthew's genealogy of Jesus. Rahab, a foreign prostitute from Jericho, is also listed as one of those four female progenitors of Jesus.

its frank and sensual admiration of sexual love and desire from both the female and male.[5] On the other hand these Scriptures also contain ghastly stories of rape and sexual license run amok, such as the story in Judges 19 of the concubine who is freely handed over to demanding male visitors and subjected to gang rape with no apparent remorse on the part of her master.

Regulating sexual behavior, especially lust, was probably a main factor behind the heavily prescriptive purity laws found in Leviticus and Deuteronomy. Efforts to protect the vulnerability of women and children are also implicit in many of the regulations of marital relations found in some law codes, though the overall effect was a strengthening of the patriarchal system so that women and children *became* male property. Even the Ten Commandments, mentioned above for outlining how Hebrew persons (both male and female) are to honor and respect God and each other, list wives as property of men in the final commandment.

Perhaps one of the most startling marriage accounts in the Hebrew Bible is that of Hosea and his wife Gomer; she is portrayed as a shameless harlot who continually betrays the faithful, forgiving love of her husband. Whatever Hosea's private pain and humiliation, in his public role as a prophet he seeks through his marriage a greater understanding of God's covenant love for humans. Hosea's story thus echoes Genesis 2 in suggesting that the purpose of marriage goes beyond procreation, beyond the patriarchal establishment of roles and responsibilities, beyond the seeking of companionship; Hosea's tale begins to hint at marriage as an opportunity for individual spiritual development that reflects God's divine nature.[6]

In summation, the Hebrew Scriptures provide varied understandings of marriage relationships. Occasional glimpses of the original understanding of male and female as created equally good and capable emerge, though the patriarchal understanding of male responsibility for provision and protection eventually develop into male dominance and even ownership of the female, enforced by religious law. Possibilities of marriage for companionship and developing spiritual maturity are also represented in the stories of the Hebrew patriarchs and matriarchs.

5. See Brubaker, *Bible and Human Sexuality.*
6. Lawler, "Marriage in the Bible," 11.

Marriage in the New Testament Gospels

The writers of the New Testament understood Jesus coming into the world of first-century Judaism as the Son of God, bringing with him a fresh revelation of God's original purposes behind established practices, many of which had become corrupted over time. Though the New Testament records very few sayings of Jesus about marriage itself, those sayings indicate that his reflections on the marital practices of his day were integral to his campaign "not to abolish the Law and the Prophets . . . but to fulfill them" (Matt 5:17), that is, to clarify and reframe the essence of the sacred teaching for the contemporary situation of first-century Judaism.

Marriage was a well-established part of patriarchal Jewish society at the time that Jesus lived and had his ministry. As the accepted conduit for control for sexual relations and social stability, marriage was considered essential for carrying on the father's name and even for the continuation of the mission of the Jewish nation. As such, marriage was expected for all those who had reached puberty.[7] The fact that Jesus was unmarried when he began his ministry (usually assumed to be about age thirty) would have been highly unusual. This anomaly continues to raise questions from persons of other faith traditions: How can there be a proper Christian understanding of marriage if the religion's founder did not himself marry? For Jesus, and indeed for the apostle Paul, who carried Jesus' message far and wide but was also not known to be married, there were other more pressing concerns than sexual relations: knowing, proclaiming, and establishing God's kingdom of love and justice on earth. Both Jesus and Paul knew the time was short for the task before them; rather than focus on a single human relationship for themselves, they committed all their efforts to spreading the message of God's love and mercy for all persons, to all persons, an understanding of personal worth that went beyond sexuality and the ability to procreate.

The New Testament presents Jesus practicing and preaching a theology which embraced all persons (neighbors) as created equally, deserving respect, and capable of knowing and understanding God's love. He especially reached out to those whom society had ignored or relegated into obscurity, including the weak, those with disease, the vulnerable ones, the outcasts, children, and women. Through his words and actions, Jesus demonstrated an acceptance of women as full persons in their own rights rather than only

7. Mackin, "Primitive Christian Understanding of Marriage," 23.

in their roles as wives. Particularly in John's Gospel, he engages in deep theological conversation with apparently unmarried women such as sisters Mary and Martha, as well as the Samaritan woman who declares herself unmarried when he asks. His words and actions reveal his understanding that women are capable of personal autonomy, societal integration, and spiritual maturity on their own.

This theology of equality, which contradicts the existing assumption that women were totally reliant on their husbands for not only their well-being but also their personal identity, raises perplexing questions for Jesus' contemporaries, both his followers and his detractors. One of the few recorded times when Jesus speaks about marriage is in response to the religious leaders of the day who question him specifically about divorce. In the Matthew 19 passage, the authorities are ostensibly asking about adherence to the precedents of Mosaic Law, but Jesus takes the opportunity to expand their understanding of the original theology of God's creation of humanity. He directs them back to the Genesis 1 account where God created humans "male and female," perhaps to remind his listeners of the original shared goodness of human creation. Jesus then recalls the well-known passage about the two leaving their homes to be joined as "one flesh," emphasizing marriage as a relationship of equality and companionship rather than a mere legal contract that could be undone on a whim.

At this point, Jesus' own (male) disciples wonder if marriage is such a good idea after all (Matt 19:10). British Methodist scholar Sheryl Anderson posits: "Jesus seems to be arguing that a wife is not piece of property and as such cannot be disowned."[8] If marriage is not about male ownership and control, then the disciples consider perhaps it's better not to marry at all. Jesus' response indicates that one's ability to love God, one's neighbor, and oneself is more important than one's marital status. For those who do marry, this most intimate and long-term relationship can become a most effective conduit for learning to love as one's neighbor (i.e., spouse) as oneself. Here Jesus is offering the marriage relationship not just as the joining of equals but as an opportunity for mutual faithfulness and maturity.

Marriage in Paul's Letters

The apostle Paul continued to expand Jesus' teaching of love and acceptance and forgiveness into practical theology for an even wider audience. His

8. Anderson, "Towards a Methodist Theology," 4.

many letters, sent to fledgling churches around the known world, spread these concepts in places where they often came into sharp conflict with local practices. Paul himself struggled to put many of Jesus' teachings into practice when they came in conflict with the strict Jewish religious instruction he had received; the role of women is a case in point. Throughout the history of the Christian church, conservative and progressive theologians disagree on whether Paul was simply misogynist, a theological complementarian who tried to balance gender roles in the household and society with practical consideration of reproductive functions, or a radical reinterpreter of Judaic law and practice who greatly enhanced female participation in society.

In Paul's first letter to the Corinthians (7:2–4), he specifies the marriage relationship as providing a healthy outlet for sexual relations and thereby reducing sexual immorality,[9] concurring with most traditional theologies of marriage. Interestingly, Paul also specifically gives both the husband and the wife the right to "rule over" the body of the other, rather than assuming only the husband rules over his wife's body. In this he is beginning to suggest some of the equality of gender roles which he expands in his letter to the Ephesians (5:22—6:9). Paul is, in effect, rewriting the Jewish Household Code to assert that the marriage relationship should be a place for practicing Jesus' teaching on how humans are to live with each other with mutual love and respect and thus honor God. More specifically in his letter to the Ephesians, Paul effectively subverts the patriarchal understanding of marriage as a wife being completely subordinate to her husband by exhorting husbands to love and be subject to their wives, again outlining his understanding that all are to "be subject to one another out of reverence for Christ" (5:21).

In his letter to the Galatians, Paul goes on to declare: "There is no longer Jew or Greek, there is no longer slave or free, there is no longer male and female; for all of you are one in Christ Jesus" (3:28). Here Paul is negotiating an understanding that being "one in Christ" is the ultimate relationship through which all other relationships are negotiated in a spirit of love and respect. Coming from this new theological perspective, many of the passages from Paul's letters would have sounded radically egalitarian to a first-century audience even if they sometimes sound restrictive to modern ears. When speaking directly of marriage, Paul, like Jesus, also refers to the

---

9. Interpreters of Paul's writings have differing opinions of whether Paul himself was fully supportive of sexual relations, even within marriage.

marital formula of "leaving home" and "becoming one flesh," but he goes on to liken marriage to the coming together of Christ and the church, each caring for and serving the other. These passages speak both of mutuality in marriage and of marriage as being a tool for developing spiritual maturity.

First Corinthians 13 is Paul's famous poem on love, by far the most common Scripture passage quoted in Christian weddings. Although Paul does not address this chapter toward married couples (he is instead addressing a squabbling church body), the passage emphasizes attitudes of accommodation for the needs and desires of the other, of being patient and kind, of not keeping track of wrong done or being envious of the other. These are qualities of Christian discipleship which married couples have abundant opportunities to practice as they pledge to love and cherish each other for better, for worse; for richer, for poorer; in sickness and in health.

Summary

From this brief overview of Judeo-Christian Scriptures, several conclusions can be drawn about the potential nature of Christian marriage:

1. The Genesis stories present God creating both male and female with inherent and equal goodness and as suitable companions for each other. The subsequent account of the fall describes punitive gender roles for each arising from their sinfulness; these contributed to prescriptive complementarian gender roles in Jewish patriarchal marriage.

2. Both Jewish and Christian understandings of marriage affirm that, while an original function of marriage was to provide healthy means for controling sexual relations, procreation is not the sole aim of the marriage relationship. Christian theology, based on Jesus' teaching and ministry as later expanded by Paul, promoted a more egalitarian understanding of gender roles in society as well as in marriage.

3. While neither Jesus nor Paul themselves were married, they recognized that marriage could be a fertile training ground for developing Christ-like love and compassion for one's partner.

CHAPTER 10

Marriage, Creation, and Gender Roles
in the Qur'an

THE ISLAMIC WORLD LOOKS to the Qur'an for spiritual and practical wisdom. This study seeks to explore the Qur'an for an Islamic understanding of how and why humans were created, their relationship with God, gender roles, the place of marriage, and how the roles of husband and wife can contribute to the spiritual development of the individual in today's world. It is important to recognize that, like virtually all faith traditions, Islam draws on several sources for its theology and practice, sources which invariably reflect customs and traditions of particular times and places. In Islam, the actual practice of the prophet Muhammad (*sunnah*), his recorded sayings (*hadith*), the scholarly interpretations of the Qur'an (*ijtihad*), and general Muslim consensus (*ijma*), are all regarded as sources for religious practice, but each must be balanced against the statements contained in the Qur'an itself. For reasons stated previously, this exploration will only use the Qur'an as an authoritative source.

The most basic premise of Islam is that humans are created to love, obey, and worship the one God, known in the Arabic as Allah. Together these attitudes toward God are known as "submission," which is the meaning of the word Islam. Allah's revelations to the prophet Muhammad, gathered into the Qur'an, form the basis for this understanding of who God is and what is required of humans. The Qur'an posits that one's love, obedience, and worship of God are wrapped up in what one *does*, particularly in following God's rule in relationship with others. In Islam, the sacred and the secular are closely intertwined, so that one's worship is seen in the way

89

one lives one's life, particularly in the life of the family, in business, and in interactions with other Muslims (*ummah*—the Muslim community) and the wider world.[1]

While nearly all contemporary Muslims avow that men and women are created equal in the sight of God, the Qur'an does not necessarily support an understanding of male and female as equal partners in marriage or society in general. Indeed, Islamic scholar Mona Siddiqi notes the challenge in "trying to translate this spiritual egalitarianism into social equalities."[2] It is important to recognize the cultural milieu to which the Qur'an was speaking, namely the highly patriarchal Bedouin tribes of the Arabian desert, where the survival of one's family and extended family unit was paramount. Marriage strengthened the chances of family and tribal survival by providing a controlled, healthy, and moral outlet for sexual relations which maintained and continued the family line. Arising out of tribal desert culture, the Qur'an also pushed against that status quo in at least three ways: presenting women as created from the same substance as men; refraining from assigning blame to women for evil; and defending the importance of providing financial and familial security to all who find themselves weak and/or vulnerable in society.

As with many traditional religious faiths, the Qur'an (and Islam) arose out of a patriarchal society in which maleness was considered the norm for humanity. The Qur'an speaks of God/Allah exclusively as male,[3] and the words of the Qur'an assume a male listener (i.e., women are referred to primarily with regards to their relationships with men). A woman must listen hard to recognize that she, too, is equally regarded in the sight of God/Allah.

Creation of Humanity

Identifying a single creation narrative in the Qur'an is challenging because the Qur'an is organized not as an unfolding story but rather a succession

---

1. Muhammad is reported to have said: "The whole world is my mosque," a phrase strikingly close to a well-loved saying of Methodist founder, John Wesley, cited in Hewer, *Understanding Islam*, 99.

2. Siddiqi, *How to Read the Qur'an*, 69.

3. Some contemporary Muslim scholars argue that God/Allah is above gender. See Barlas, *"Believing Women" in Islam*, 99–108.

of the revelations that came to the prophet Muhammad.[4] References to Adam's creation are scattered throughout several suras (Qur'anic verses); rather than attempting to explain how humans were created, these references usually serve to remind humans that they are the created ones who so often forget their Creator and are ungrateful. The Hebrew creation narratives found in Genesis were known in the Arab world and formed a loose basis for the Islamic understanding of creation, albeit with several Qur'anic corrections. In several suras, Adam is created first from clay dust; we are also told that he receives a mate with whom he lives in the garden until they disobey and are banished. There are also many references to Adam being not only created "from clay" but by "from a drop of mingled fluid" (Q 76:2, 77:20, 16:4, 23:13, 35:11)[5] just as his descendants are created, including his unnamed mate; in Q 55.14, it is a *generic* "mankind" which is created. In these latter examples, the emphasis is on humans being created "from a single soul," a phrase which hints at a created equality of humankind.

The garden narrative continues in sura 2:35 (and 7:19) with God telling Adam to "live with your wife in this garden. Both of you eat freely there as you will, but do not go near this tree, or you will both become wrongdoers."[6] Even though God is speaking only to Adam, here we find God providing equally for each of the partners and assigning moral responsibility to each. In the Qur'anic garden narrative, the Satan (*Iblis*), rather than the serpent, entices the couple to disobey, and the woman does not inherit the reputation as temptress as does the biblical Eve.

Islamic Gender Roles

These elements of sexual equality—male and female created by God from the same source; male and female provided for equally by God; both held jointly responsible for morality and their actions—are affirmed in the opening verses of sura 92: "By the covering night, by the radiant day, by the male

4. The chapters of the Qur'an are presented in order of brevity rather than chronological sequence.

5. All citations from: Haleem, *Qur'an*.

6. This is a typical feature of the Qur'an in which Allah speaks only to the male. In sura 3, however, God's angel speaks directly to Mary, who has no husband until God appoints Zachariah to care for her—though ultimately it is God who provides: "Whenever Zachariah went in to see her in her sanctuary, he found her supplied with provision. He said, 'Mary, how is it you have these provisions?' and she said, 'They are from God: God provides limitlessly for whoever he will'" (Q 3.42).

and female He created," but this is immediately clarified with the complementarian argument: "[but] the ways you take differ greatly." Indeed, Islam might best describe male/female equality in terms of "you are equal and yet you differ." Sura 3:36 clearly states "the male is not like the female." Here the physical vulnerability of the female, particularly with regards to pregnancy and childrearing, provides the rationale for treating the sexes differently. At its best this patriarchal arrangement provides protection and support for vulnerability; at its worst it becomes a tool for confining the female to a subservient role.

It is useful here to consider what other forms of humanity apart from women were deemed to need protection in the Qur'an: children, slaves, and most especially orphans.[7] The adult male was the appointed protector of such vulnerable persons within the patriarchal society, providing for his family food, clothing, housing, financial income, and protection from those who would attack from the outside. If this protection was not given, the vulnerable had little (if any) chance of surviving. Within this understanding of male protective responsibility, Muhammad sanctioned the preexisting provision for polygyny, the practice by which a male could take several wives. Muhammad approved this especially for orphan girls (Q 4:3) and widows on the understanding that they would otherwise be vulnerable and unprotected in society. He also set a limit of a man having no more than four wives, with the proviso that the husband must adequately and equally love and care for each of them, an arrangement which a later verse deems virtually impossible: "You will never be able to treat your wives with equal fairness, however much you may desire to do so" (Q 4:129).

Some in contemporary society question whether the practice of polygyny was genuinely advantageous to the female or whether it was merely an outlet for male sexual privilege. In Q 3:14, women are the at the top of a list of "desirable things . . . made alluring for men." Indeed, the Qur'an speaks of (male) lust as a major turning away from God and promotes marriage as a way in which "God wishes to lighten your burden; [for] man was created weak" (Q 4:28). Though Islam insists that sexual relations are good and wholesome for men and women, the Qur'an speaks of the male as created weak with regards to sexual control and seems to imply that the wife is primarily there to "lighten [his sexual] burden" rather than seek her own sexual fulfillment. In Q 7:189, Adam's mate is made "that he might find

---

7. Muhammad himself was an orphan and so was well aware of the vulnerability of the situation.

comfort in her"; the fact that this passage continues with a description of her becoming pregnant and giving birth, could lead one to assume that the comfort is, at least in this passage, sexual and primarily for the male. In the (in)famous description of how/why a Muslim man might reprimand his wife (Q 4:34), the husband is urged to "ignore [her] in bed." This could be interpreted as implying that sexual relations can potentially become a tool with which the husband asserts his control.

Sura 4:34 also gives the husband the option of hitting his wife, that is, resorting to physical violence to show her the error of her ways, though many contemporary scholars consider this as contrary to the general spirit of the Qur'an, and some question the meaning of the translation from Arabic.[8] The sura goes on to give a Muslim wife some recourse to the situation, suggesting that a Muslim husband might need to be reminded of his error "if a wife fears high-handedness or alienation from her husband." Her suggested recourse is to negotiate "a peaceful settlement" noting that "although human souls are prone to selfishness, if you do good and are mindful of God, He is well aware of all that you do" (Q 4:128). In any case, the squabbling pair is urged to seek arbitration with assistance from both sides of their families. "Then, if the couple want to put things right, God will bring about a reconciliation between them: He is all knowing, all aware" (Q 4:35).

In general, the Qur'an envisions good marriages in which husbands "take good care of their wives" while the "wives are devout and guard what God would have them guard in their husbands' absence" (Q 4:34). Here we have a glimpse of the male's vulnerability (i.e., that his property might be at risk while he is away from the family/tribe). The wife, then, is entrusted with covering his vulnerability, which indicates some confidence in her abilities and hints at some measure of mutuality.

As noted above, Islam assigns different roles to men and women within the family unit. Perhaps the simplest characterization would be that of outside (male) and inside (female) roles. As the husband assumes full responsibility for financial provision for his family, his energies are directed into the community (and beyond) as he works to ensure sufficient income. Because his is the outside role, he is more involved with the communal activities beyond the home, going, for instance, to the mosque for daily prayers, to the shop or business setting for work, or being a trader who must travel, or a warrior who goes to battle to protect his family and tribe. Since

8. See Barlas, *"Believing Women" in Islam,* 188, and Al-Hibri, Azizah and El Habti, "Islam," 190–91.

the secular and sacred are intimately connected with the outside realm, the political/religious leader for the community (i.e., the *imam*) must be male.

Meanwhile, the female's responsibility is inside, that is, primarily within the home, seeing to the practical provision of homemaking and childbearing. The Muslim woman's only specified duty is a willingness to bear children, with nursing and even raising her children being tasks that can reasonably be delegated to another (Q 2:233). She prays at home and is responsible for ensuring for the practice of *salat* at home, that is, teaching the children to pray and obey Islamic practices. She is responsible for providing *halal* foods, prohibiting alcoholic drinks, and observing modesty in her dress and demeanor. Beyond household responsibilities, she can and should be educated and have her own money and income for which she is solely accountable.

The inside and outside nature of the roles Islam has assigned to women and men have resulted in an interesting anomaly with regards to interfaith marriage. Muslim men can marry Christians or Jews as these are "people of the Book," but there is no provision for Muslim women to marry outside Islam. Some believe this originally stems from the practice of Muslim men who often had to travel or live at long distances from their familial/tribal homes to engage in commerce, education, or warfare; because there might not be a suitable Muslim woman available in such places to become his wife, he could marry out. The Muslim woman, however, would not travel outside her home, so she would be restricted to marrying the Muslim men in her area.[9]

Islam in general assumes that all adult Muslims will marry since sexual activity is regarded as healthy and necessary. Apart from the sexual aspect, the Qur'an also endorses marriage with these words: "And the [married] believers, men and women, are protecting friends one of another; they enjoin the right and forbid the wrong, and they establish worship and they pay the poor-due, and they obey Allah and His messenger" (Q 9:71). Q 2:187 speaks of husband and wife being "garments" for each other, "that is, one who covers the other's shortcoming and protects his or her privacy."[10] This passage gives further insights into the covering of vulnerability that was mentioned earlier. Not only are husband and wife protecting the other

---

9. Some Muslim traditions understand the prohibition to be based on a belief that a child would be raised in the father's religion, thus ensuring the continuity of the faith tradition.

10. Al-Hibri and El Habti, "Islam," 177.

from the vulnerabilities to which their roles and responsibilities expose them, his in the business world, hers in the domestic arena, they protect each other's vulnerability in the private world. This confirms that Islam also values the emotional gratification, personal support, and spiritual growth that can come from the close companionship of a man and woman living, loving, and working together.

Summary

In many ways, the postmodern world—with its easy access to birth control, a preponderance of couples choosing to cohabit rather than marry, a heightened awareness of domestic abuse, and women's increased activity in outside activities—poses challenges to the Islamic understandings of marriage based primarily on traditional Arabic culture.[11] In the face of these challenges, some in Islam (as in other religions) have resorted to absolute adherence to traditional practices without thoughtful attention to the theological tenets behind them. Yet others continue the long Islamic tradition of reexamining the tradition in light of contemporary reality, especially wrestling with theological principles from the Qur'an which will further develop perspectives of equality of the sexes that can serve the present age:

1. Marriage provides fertile ground for Islamic men and women seeking to perfect their own submission to Allah; through their day-to-day relationship they can learn from each other about submitting their own needs and wants to those of their spouse.

2. Trust is an essential element of any successful partnership, and trust ensues when each knows the other will be acting in morally responsible ways. A Muslim husband or wife who puts the love of God first and foremost in his or her life will be one who also treats other persons with respect as all persons are created equally before God.

3. Islam understands God's will as insisting that protection is provided for the vulnerable. Apart from the vulnerability of women during pregnancy, childbirth, and child-rearing, there is a growing realization that men also have times of vulnerability. Both husbands and wives have mutual responsibilities to care for each other, particularly

---

11. The legality of homosexual marriage is also a contemporary challenge for Islam, but that issue is outside the remit of this book.

when the other is vulnerable. Marriage becomes a partnership for protecting the other.

4. While many of the restraints of the patriarchal tribe could be considered nonapplicable to today's world, certainly the partnership of a wife and husband seeking to establish a viable family life which protects children and other extended family members provides an important unit of stability for society at large.

5. The traditional sole responsibility of the husband to provide financially for the family might be challenged in light of women's increased ability to earn income by working outside the home. Contemporary reality would press the theological implications of husband and wife sharing financial responsibility for the family.

Finally, even as the concept of marriage solely in terms of sexual provision and protection may seem outdated, many postmodern couples are attracted to the deeper spiritual, emotional, and intellectual growth that can occur when women and men join for the long haul of marriage. With regard to the marriage relationship, sura 30 includes in its description of why praise is due to God: "He created spouses from among yourselves for you to live with in tranquillity: He ordered love and kindness between you" (Q 30:21). That is a timeless aspiration for Muslims and all married couples.

CHAPTER 11

Marriage and Spiritual Growth
in Hindu Scripture

THE HINDUISM OF TODAY is a rich patchwork tapestry of daily routines, social customs, and faith traditions stitched together over millennia. It reveals ancient customs which sustained people groups living in the Indus Valley and evolved over subsequent ages as they came in contact with traders, explorers, and conquerors who brought with them other faith practices and social conventions.[1] A multiplicity of worship traditions and beliefs emerged, centered around local (and adopted) deities and tribal patterns, each seeking a path to spiritual maturity. Elaborate stories of gods and goddesses were passed down orally through the generations, rich mythical accounts of divine activity informing human sensibilities. This diversity of sources and practices makes the task of determining a *single* Hindu theology of human creation and how one is to live as a Hindu—or a married person—very challenging indeed.

Still, Hinduism presents a surprisingly unified understanding of the human problem it seeks to address: how to break free from the cycle of life, death, and rebirth known as *samsara,* a cycle which prevents humans from attaining their true spiritual liberation of complete unity with God.[2] Hindus also agree that humanity was created from the goodness of divine truth with the intent of humanity continuing in that blissful state of divine unity. Unfortunately, humans often make bad decisions which result in suffering.

1. Smith, *World's Religions,* 72. Smith lists "Jains, Buddhists, Parsees, Muslims, Sikhs, and Christians" as the main contributors to the Hindu religious dialogue.

2. Prothero, *God Is Not One,* 136.

Karma is the Hindu understanding that each action has a cause and effect and that these causes and effects follow a person from one life into the next (reincarnation) until one is finally released to return to the divine state known as *moksha,* or complete union with the divine.

The ultimate goal of *moksha* can be attained through following one of three *yogas* (disciplines): *jnana* (wisdom), *karma* (action), or *bhakti* (love and devotion for one's god). Apart from *moksha,* there are three aims in life for Hindus: *kama,* sensual pleasure; *artha,* the gaining of wealth and power; and *dharma,* duty in the sense of doing that which is good and right and true.[3] Hindu philosophy posits that there are different stages of life (*asramas*) during which one pursues one or another of these aims more intently. As a *brahmacharya* (student), one's main responsibility is to learn and obey (*jnana*). As a *grihastha* (householder), one should marry and establish a family and a household; during this period, one's primary duty is to gain the wealth and power (*artha*) needed to support one's family, but *kama sutra,* that is, sexual enjoyment, is also expected. In later life, one's journey toward *moksha* provides the incentive to give up personal attachments in order to live a life of pure reflection on God, perhaps even becoming a *vanaprastha* (forest dweller). At a final stage, one may become a *sanyasi,* giving up one's name and personal identity as well as all other attachments, though this might not happen until a future (reincarnated) life.

Early on, Hinduism established a highly organized social structure which included clearly defined roles for men and women, as well as class delineations (caste). The overriding framework of patriarchy can be recognized in the observation that the traditional life stages are described primarily in male terms, with the female usually allowed (or expected) to follow/accompany her husband. Patriarchy at its best ensures that women, especially in the periods of life when they are most vulnerable, are cared for by men. Patriarchy at its worst condemns women to the complete control and exploitation of men.[4] As our purpose is to tease out perspectives from

3. Prothero, *God Is Not One,* 137.

4. An interesting anomaly to the overriding patriarchal framework sometimes occurs in the ubiquitous Mangala Pherā (fire ceremony) of traditional Hindu weddings where the *female* takes the lead in going around the fire for the first three out of four circumnavigations: "which signifies that woman are more mature and grown up emotionally and physically, are capable of making greater sacrifices, and have put in more efforts to learn the responsibility of the future family life, adjust to the new family . . . to keep harmony among all, to bear and raise children, and to learn the family traditions including the following: internal management within the means of the family's earning ability, interpersonal relationships, and hosting the friends and guests" (Courtright,

faith traditions that are useful in a twenty-first-century egalitarian society, we will pursue Hindu traditions and stories that give glimpses of male and female roles within marriage which support the flourishing and mutual protection and support of both.

Creation of Humanity and Gendered Divinity

As we explore social and marital roles for male and female from the Hindu creation narratives, we must appreciate that, for Hindus, the origin of the world and its inhabitants is of secondary importance to an understanding that the true essence of a human being *(Atman)* is divine *(Brahman)* and therefore *uncreated*, deathless, and immortal.[5] Human life as experienced on earth is not the ultimate reality, only a passing phase toward *moksha*. More essential is an understanding of the gods and goddesses and their creation stories which present the fundamental (nonhuman) essence of divinity as a co-existence of male and female, represented in various divine pairings such as Shiva and Shakti or (female) Saraswati and (male) Brahma.

In the Upanishad account, Shiva and Shakti are recognized as the divine Father and Mother: "Shiva is the eternal Spirit, the Absolute, represented as dwelling aloof on the mountain peak of spiritual peace. Shakti, the Divine Mother, is his creative partner, and without her, Shiva could never have created the world . . . Thus, it is in the union of Shiva and Shakti that all things are born."[6]

In this Vishnu tradition, Shiva is the *purusha*, or essential purity of consciousness of Self, understood as male, and Shakti is the *prakriti*, the energy or matter, usually understood as female, encompassing birth and death. It is often stressed that male and female are not the best ways to describe this Self/energy dynamic, and yet this perspective provides a clue for exploring the essential unity of the two: "without energy Self is practically immovable and without Self energy does not have any field for its movements."[7]

In the tantric traditions of Hinduism, Shiva and Shakti are again regarded as male and female energy poles, two complementary forces which,

---

"Hinduism," 284).

    5. Prothero, *God Is Not One*, 149.

    6. Easwaran, *Bhagavad Gita*, 214.

    7. Jayaram, "Hinduism," para. 17.

when combined, unleash explosive energy.[8] This tantric tradition is firmly rooted in male/female sexual relations, understood to be powerful agents for attaining spiritual awareness. The female, variously portrayed as Shakti, Kali, or Parvati, is recognized as the Creator, the initiator who energizes the spiritual realm of Shiva and brings matter to birth. Kali, in her fully awakened ferocious state with blood-red tongue, stands with her foot on Shiva, triumphant; Parvati is sometimes pictured as seated below Shiva as his disciple, receiving his spiritual instruction. In other portrayals Shiva is sucking at the breast of Shakti; sometimes Shiva's body is pictured as half male and half female. In the tantric tradition, the female is the spiritual leader, as she is more in tune with emotions and therefore more aware of spiritual matters than the male. In the Vedic tradition, the Shiva/Shakti, *purusha/prakriti* concepts present an understanding of male and female as integral parts of the essence of life, both being and doing.

The Hindu scriptures, with their plethora of male and female deities, depict God as male and female, merciful as well as vengeful, Mother as well as Father, as passionate lover, wise friend, even mischievous child.[9] In the best-known Hindu scripture, the *Bhagavad Gita,* Krishna is the male *avatar* with no mention of a female counterpart. Krishna rather claims all the divine attributes, even those such as birth and death which we have seen described as the qualities of Shakti's *prakriti*: "I [Krishna] am death, which overcomes all, and the source of all being still to be born" (Gita 10:34). The verse goes on to name the feminine qualities which Krishna claims as divine: "fame, beauty, perfect speech, memory, intelligence, loyalty, and forgiveness." The fact that these feminine qualities are considered part of the male *avatar* can either be interpreted as acknowledging female aspects of the divinity or as indicating that the female is subsumed within the larger male divinity. In each interpretation is a recognition that intelligence and beauty can be considered both female and male, and that both are created with the potential for divine goodness.

Marriage in Hinduism

Within Hinduism, marriage is subsumed within the ultimate importance of *family*. Indeed, Hindus would agree that family is the framework for continuity and well-being in communal and personal life, and that marriage is

8. Saraswati, "Role of Women in Tantra," para. 3.

9. Morrison, "Introduction to Chapter Twelve," 204.

the primary relationship which makes family possible. Within that context of family and marriage, sex is "the embodied difference between human beings as male and female that find[s] physical pleasure, companionship, and duration in the context of family and society."[10]

Continuing the family line, especially producing a male offspring, is the way in which ancestors are honored and their descendants ensured a chance to attain *moksha*. A son is considered to be the replica of his father, and so responsibility for furthering the family's spiritual progression is passed on to a new generation. The husband and wife producing a son have therefore completed the essential responsibility of the second (householder) stage of life, continued their own spiritual progression, and fulfilled their first and foremost obligation to their family line.

Regulations to govern marital relations, including detailed requirements of *dharma* for husbands and wives, were enshrined in the Laws of Manu (ca. 100 BCE—200 CE), known as the *Manusmriti*.[11] These Laws were built on a primitive understanding from agriculture: the wife was the field and the husband was the seed. In this context, the inability of a wife to produce a male child was a defect of the field, so another wife should be brought in to ensure continuity of the family line.[12] These concepts of field and seed also served to regulate sexual relationships: a husband was responsible for—and the rightful recipient of—the seed planted in his own field, but neither should he plant his seed in another man's field: the resulting offspring would be his responsibility but could not be counted to his own credit. Indeed, the Gita understood lust as male sexual desire for a woman who is not one's wife and declared it one of the "three gates to . . . self-destructive hell" (Gita, 16:21).

As one's spiritual progression depended on producing offspring, Hindu marriage provided the framework for that to happen. We noted earlier that, particularly during the householder stage of life, sex within marriage was to be enjoyed as *kama*, a sensual pleasure and one of the aims of human life. In short, sexual relations and sexual pleasure within marriage are encouraged in Hinduism. Hinduism also preserves an understanding of sexual relations as divine, with the potential for better appreciating divine

---

10. Courtright, "Hinduism," 229.

11. *The Laws of Manu,* cited in Courtright, "Hinduism," 240–49.

12. According to the Kamasutra 4.2.2, the barren wife has the responsibility to urge her husband to take a co-wife (Cited in Courtright, "Hinduism," 252).

love by cultivating an intimate human connection, especially through sexual interactions.[13]

With regard to personal spiritual development, the question remains as to whether marriage as a vehicle for healthy sexual relations (and thus better understanding divine love) is still needed in the third or fourth stage of life when the aim of drawing closer to God is to be facilitated by renouncing human attachments. The Gita says of those maturing spiritually: "Free from selfish attachment, they do not get compulsively entangled even in home and family" (Gita 13:9). This could be understood as advising one to leave one's family in pursuit of complete unity with the divine, though most Hindus would assume this might only happen later in life after one's procreative duties are complete. On the other hand the Gita also claims, "When a person responds to the joys and sorrows of others as if they were his own, he has attained the highest state of spiritual union" (Gita 6:32), so remaining in a close and loving relationship with one's spouse could also be a way of attaining *moksha*.

Also embedded in Hindu marital relations is an obligation for both husband and wife to "protect" the other.[14] Husbands are to protect their wives from outside danger and temptations; wives are to protect their husbands by ensuring their physical and emotional needs are provided for within the home. Both are to protect the relationship by remaining faithful and supportive. Faithfulness and support within the marriage relationship can also provide protection for both in terms of personal development and for society in terms of social stability.

Raama and Seetha—The Ideal Hindu Husband and Wife

A consideration of marriage as companionship that results in *moksha* leads us to the *Ramayana,* Hinduism's greatest love story.[15] The ancient saga of the royal prince Raama and his beautiful and devoted wife Seeta reveals much about Hindu understandings of the role of husband and wife and their relationship to each other. In brief, the story tells of Prince Raama being banished from his kingdom when his father, King Dasaratha, is tricked by one of his wives into making her own son king in place of the rightful

13. Prothero, *God Is Not One,* 155.

14. Courtright, "Hinduism," 230.

15. Rajagopalachari, *Ramayana.* Subsequent citations from the *Ramayana* will be indicated by an "R," followed by the page number in this edition.

prince, Raama. Raama, fully understanding his duty (*dharma*) to obey his father, agrees to the banishment. To his surprise, Seeta, his wife of twelve years, also insists on following him in his banishment to the forest as does Raama's half-brother, Lakshmana. After ten of their fourteen years of banishment has passed, Seeta is kidnapped by an evil god/king who takes her to his kingdom of Lanka. Eventually the monkey god Hanuman rescues her on behalf of Raama while Raama is fighting an apocalyptic battle in Lanka for Seeta.

Though great emphasis has been made of Raama's love for Seeta (and hers for him), near the end of the saga, Raama shuns Seeta for having lived "too long" in another man's house (during her captivity). Seeta protests this unjust attitude of Raama's by consigning herself to a funeral pyre through which her innocence is duly demonstrated as she emerges unscathed. Raama then claims he was testing her so that everyone would know they were both righteous. The story ends with the couple reunited—happily ever after? As Raama and Seeta are regarded as the ideal Hindu husband and wife, we will explore the *Ramayana* for clues on these ideals.

Gender Roles in the *Ramayana*

Raama is a prince, a king-in-waiting in social status, and a *kshatriya* (warrior) by caste. The *Ramayana* paints him as an ideal husband, one who fully knows and carries out his duty, his *dharma,* to protect and provide for his people, and particularly his wife. As Protector, he fights (and wins) epic battles against tremendous odds and circumstances. As Provider, Raama is eager to ensure the best possible circumstances for Seeta, even when they are living in the forest, completely cut off from worldly comforts. Raama loves his wife and admires her beauty immensely; he is heart-sick when he realizes she has been taken from him. His admiration for her fails only near the end of the story when he appears to doubt her integrity.

Seeta is the ideal wife, "the embodiment of compassion and grace" (R, 310). When her father, King Janaka, presents her on their wedding day, he proclaims to Raama: "Here is my daughter, Seeta, who will ever tread with you the path of *dharma*. Take her hand in yours. Blessed and devoted, she will ever walk with you like your own shadow" (R, 310). Indeed, this saying has been an important part of wedding ceremonies in India for countless generations. Raama becomes the complete focus of Seeta's wifely attention and devotion regardless of her circumstances; she even insists on following him into the forest of his banishment: "As for Seeta, there in the forest, as here in the palace, she lives for Raama with every breath and knows neither fear nor sorrow" (R, 93).

Seeta's physical beauty is frequently mentioned in the *Ramayana*; even when describing her as the "perfect embodiment of wifely virtues," the narrator goes on to speak of "beautiful garments and auspicious cosmetics that set out the charms of lovely young wives" (R, 126). But lest one conclude that her beauty was only skin-deep, Seeta's actions also speak of the inner qualities of devotion and compassion, particularly for her husband. Seeta continually reminds Raama, through her actions as well as words, that she shares with him a firm commitment to *dharma*. "You and I must tread together the path of *dharma*. How can we differ?" (R, 132). In this way, she becomes something of a spiritual guide for her husband. As they travel through the forest, she is the one who frequently prays to the forest deities for their safety and success in fulfilling their *dharma*. While she relies on Raama (and brother-in-law Lakshmana) for protection and rescue, she is also portrayed as one who can think for herself and who is curious and admiring of the world around her.

Other husbands and wives figure in the *Ramayana*, but nearly all the story's action is initiated by males. The notable exception is performed early in the story by Kaikeyi, the wife of Dasaratha, who agrees to a scheme concocted by a female servant of hers to put Kaikeyi's son, Bharata, on the royal throne instead of Raama, the assumed primogeniture. Kaikeyi's treachery is portrayed as especially cruel as she had been Dasaratha's favorite: "Of all his consorts, Kaikeyi was the one whose company he sought for joyous relaxation from all cares of state, for she never interfered in public affairs, and always waited for him at the entrance and welcomed him with a warm embrace" (R, 58). Here are clues that the ideal wife should be concerned primarily with making her husband's private life comfortable and staying out of his public life. Indeed, Raama's own mother knows her wifely duty was "to serve her husband in his old age and share his sorrow" (R, 74).

Another exceptional woman in the *Ramayana* is Taara, wife of king Vaali. As he lies dying, Vaali himself beseeches those who remain: "And be kind to Taara who was not only a blameless and affectionate wife, but also a very wise and far-sighted counselor . . . Do not disregard her advice on any matter" (R, 192). Surprising for modern ears, the story continues with Taara pleading for her husband's killer to kill her as well: "Even in heaven, he will not be happy without me. Do not fear it would be a sin. It will be a meritorious act to unite husband and wife. This will cleanse your sin, your treacherous slaying of my husband" (R, 192). Taara is, in fact, spared this death, and in the process wins through her statesmanship "the compassion and sympathy of all" (R, 194). The narrator continues: "In looks, in knowledge of the world and skill in speech, Taara was unrivalled" (R, 197). High praise, indeed!

Companionship in Marriage

Returning to the marital relationship between Raama and Seeta, we find an oft-repeated theme of ideal love and fidelity: "Raama . . . surrendered his heart to Seeta. It was difficult for one to say whether their love grew because of their virtues or it was planted in their beauty of form. Their hearts communed even without speech. Seeta, rejoicing in Raama's love, shone like Lakshmi in heaven" (R, 47).

Seeta describes her husband as "a perfect being. His love for me equals mine for him. His affection is unchanging. Pure of heart, he has mastered the senses" (R, 47). Particularly interesting in the context of this ideal Hindu marriage, though, is the absence of offspring, even after Raama and Seeta's twenty-plus years together. Indeed, there is no mention of sexual relations between the two during the twelve years that they lived together in the forest, constantly accompanied by his brother Lakshmana. If the lack of offspring were due to infertility, surely the couple were aware of the well-established practice of royal men taking additional wives to ensure the continuity of their dynasty: Raama and Lakshmana are half-brothers because their father took additional wives when his first wives did not produce offspring. The point of this highly anachronistic situation could be that their mutual love was sufficient to validify the marriage, or perhaps this is merely a story to illustrate a divine principle, that of self-giving love to another.

Indeed, the love story of the *Ramayana* is extremely idealized. As an exiled prince, Raama's work within the marriage was solely to protect and provide for Seeta, though in reality most of the daily tasks of providing for her seem to have been delegated to his brother Lakshmana. As a member of the *Kshatriya* caste, Raama's *dharma* to protect Seeta makes strenuous demands of his warrior skills, but his skills are also highly idealized. Meanwhile, without children to care for and having Lakshmana on hand to do all the household chores in the forest, Seeta's work appears to consist completely of keeping Raama happy. When she is kidnapped and taken away to Lanka, her role is wait for her husband and keep herself chaste. She famously succeeds in this task, so much so that Hanuman, the monkey god who assists in securing her eventual rescue, claims, "Seeta has saved herself. She [even] saved me, for it was her purity and power that kept the fire from harming me. How can fire help paying homage to the goddess of Chastity?" (R, 247–48).

The *Ramayana* goes on to compare Seeta's ideal chaste love for Raama with the compassion of God's love for humans. As such, attempts at assigning a hierarchy to male/female roles in human or divine love fall apart. Seeta is portrayed as "the female counterpart of the Supreme Being . . . the embodiment of compassion and grace. Compassion is the Supreme Mother and she is enthroned in the heart of the Lord" (R, 310). The passage goes on to declare the unity of "God as Father and God as Mother" claiming that separating the Supreme Mother's compassion from God's person (Father?) would be like separating Seeta from Raama. The gist of the argument is that "the quality of the Lord's compassion can be understood from the experience of true human love" (R, 310). This passage provides an argument for Hindu marriage being a path toward spiritual maturity.

The tantric tradition has an addendum to the story of Seeta and Raama in which Seeta becomes pregnant in her old age (at which time Raama was over sixty).[16] She goes to live in an ashram while Raama continues his kingly duties, which at one point require him to perform a religious ceremony. The religious elders decree that he is forbidden to carry out the religious rite without his wife present, a situation happily remedied by creating a statue of Seeta which sits beside Raama during the ceremony. This interpretation highlights several essential principles in Hindu marriage: that the marital relationship of Seeta and Raama is blessed by procreation, that the female presence is required in the sacred realm, and that both male and female are integral to the proper functioning of society.

Interfaith Marriage

Though Hinduism itself has historically been open to embracing a wide variety of cultural and faith differences, it has usually done so from a position of adopting rather than adapting (i.e., the foreign tradition would be incorporated within Hinduism). With regard to marriage, though, the

16. Saraswati, "The Role of Women in Tantra," para. 11.

previous discussion of the importance within Hindu marriage of producing offspring to carry on the family line's spiritual progression remains paramount. Marrying someone from one's own caste (or possibly above) was important as one's offspring was considered the replica of oneself in spiritual as well as physical terms. In climbing the spiritual ladder toward *moksha*, one's caste should not be jeopardized by one's offspring being from a lower caste; indeed, the whole family's spiritual progress was at stake. The same caste mindset would apply to marrying someone from another religion as well. This understanding has led to a great reluctance of Hindu families to endorse interfaith marriages.

Additionally, the understanding that the spiritual progression of the family depended upon their offspring has meant that whole families undertook the responsibility to find a suitable spouse for their children, hence the practice of arranged marriages. Though the practice has been much maligned and misunderstood in the contemporary world, it is built on the premise that parents are in the best position to understand what their child needs in a marriage partner and to do their utmost to find a suitable spouse. The young person would not have to be tempted by infatuation that might obscure their true assessment of finding a suitable life-partner. Each party assumed that a compatible couple would and could in time also learn to love each other. Indeed, in most contemporary arranged marriages, compatibility is a prime concern, and the prospective bride and groom each have the opportunity to meet and get to know each other (and their families) and give their consent before a marriage is agreed to. From that perspective, "love marriages," as they are known, continue to be frowned upon in Hindu culture, and the argument for an interfaith marriage because a couple has fallen in love is given little credence.

Contemporary Hindu Marriage

Hindu wedding ceremonies are well known for taking place over several days, each day's segment having a separate purpose. Though wedding traditions within Hinduism vary, many include an ancient rite called the *satapadi*, or "Seven Steps," in which the bridal couple circle the traditional *Agni* (nuptial fire), making seven promises to each other:

> With God as our guide,
> let us take the first step to nourish each other;
> the second step to grow together in strength;

the third step to preserve our wealth;
the fourth step to share our joys and sorrows;
the fifth step to care for our children;
the sixth step to be together forever;
the seventh step to remain lifelong friends,
the perfect halves to make a perfect whole.[17]

This set of promises confirms the intent of Hindu marriage as mutual support and holding each other accountable to high standards of fidelity and personal growth.

Summary

The Hindu institution of marriage seeks to provide strong family units in which spiritual maturity can be experienced and passed on from one generation to the next. Like other traditions of marriage, it probably emerged from a need to manage sexual relations within a patriarchal society and thus provide stability for society and protection for the vulnerable. Hindu marriage also proves itself capable of fostering a relationship in which each partner may learn more about human love and compassion from his or her partner and thus develop into a more complete person. That close human companionship can, in turn, enable each to progress to the *moksha* of complete devotion to God.

As understandings of human reproduction have moved on from the ancient concepts of seed and field, contemporary Hindus can wrestle with concepts such as whether marriage would still be capable of nurturing spiritual maturity for a couple which could not, or elected not to, have children. Is a childless Hindu marriage still a blessing?

17. "Satapadi (Seven Steps)," lines 4–13.

CHAPTER 12

Marriage and Human Relationships in Buddhism

BY ELIZABETH HARRIS

BUDDHISM AROSE IN NORTHEAST INDIA in the fifth century BCE with the teaching of the historical Buddha, Siddhartha Gautama, at a time when philosophical debate about the meaning of life and the nature of the human person was vibrant. Teaching that the suffering, pain, and disease that surround human existence were caused by our ignorance and egocentric craving, the Buddha laid out a spiritual path that aimed at eliminating this craving and its fuel, namely the three poisons of greed, hatred, and delusion. The foundation of this path was faith in the Buddha's teaching and morality. Added to this were forms of mental culture or meditation, the development of compassion and the cultivation of insight into the nature of existence. The goal was liberation from suffering, nirvana, a state characterized by wisdom and compassion, which Buddhists believe was supremely present in the perfectly enlightened Buddha, Siddhartha.

The Buddha's teaching was nontheistic in that no place was given within it to a creator-God. Sentient beings, according to Buddhism, were not created by a divinity. Rather, because they had not eradicated their greed, hatred, and delusion, they were locked in an incredibly long process of rebirth within different planes, including hells, the animal world, heavens, and the human state. Nirvana was release from this imprisonment, release from rebirth. Within this cosmology, however, birth as a human was considered to be positive, because it gave beings the best chance to progress spiritually toward nirvana. To this day, therefore, Buddhists see human life as infinitely precious and as the gateway to liberation/nirvana, if used well.

The Fourfold Community of Buddhism

In a teaching career that is traditionally seen to have lasted for over forty years, the Buddha built up a fourfold community of followers comprised of male and female monastics, and lay men and lay women. Those who joined the Buddha's monastic communities left their home and families and followed a disciplinary rule that enjoined strict celibacy and the loosening of ties with their biological families. A monastic who had sex with another human or an animal faced expulsion from his or her monastic community.[1] Barred from marriage, Buddhist monastics, therefore, found their family within their communities of monks or nuns, their rule of discipline enjoining an ethic of mutual accountability.

This monastic ideal was prioritized in the early centuries of Buddhism. Because they were free from the attachments present in lay life that fostered egocentric craving, monks and nuns were considered to be on the fast track to nirvana. One early text within the Pali Canon—a collection of texts that still unites Theravada Buddhists in countries such as Cambodia, Myanmar, Sri Lanka, and Thailand—elevates the aloneness of monasticism above familial relationships: "The attachment toward children and wives is like a bamboo clump thickly grown and entangled. Being, therefore, free from entanglement like the new bamboo tip, let one live alone like a unicorn's horn."[2]

Eventually, two broad forms of monasticism emerged: 1) monastics who lived in monasteries that were situated close to lay communities in towns and villages, and provided services for them such as preaching, funeral rituals, counseling, and chanting protective texts, and 2) forest monastics, who tended to be more isolated, with a greater focus on meditation and individual spiritual practice.

---

1. The Buddhist monastic discipline followed today is largely found in the *Vinaya Piṭaka* of the Pali Canon, the collection of texts that unites Theravada Buddhists.

2. *Khaggavisāṇa Sutta* (The Unicorn's Horn), *The Sutta Nipāta* v. 38 (Saddhatissa, 5).

Lay Communities in Buddhism

All monastic communities, however, were dependent on lay people for their food and other requisites, such as monastic robes, alms-bowls and gifts of land for monasteries. Lay communities of men and women, therefore, became central to the development of Buddhism as donors. One three-fold categorization of lay practice in Theravada Buddhist countries places generosity (interpreted as generosity to Buddhist monastics) in first place, followed by morality and meditation. Within the category of morality, five ethical precepts became central to lay practice: to abstain from harming any living being; to abstain from taking what is not given; to abstain from sexual misconduct; to abstain from false speech; and to abstain from taking substances/intoxicants that cloud the mind (often interpreted as alcohol, but in essence much wider than this). These are still held dear by Buddhist communities today. As for meditation, one important practice for lay Buddhists has always been meditation on lovingkindness, in which meditators imagine lovingkindness stretching from their minds and hearts to teachers, friends, neighbors, and eventually their enemies.

Marriage in Buddhism

The third precept, to abstain from sexual misconduct, has been interpreted in various ways in the history of Buddhism. Most interpretations start, however, with the assumption that marriage is foundational to maintaining harmony within lay society. Single women were traditionally considered to be unrestrained and in need of marriage![3] The earliest textual definitions of the precept mention refraining from going to the wife of another, namely refraining from adultery, with the "moral subject" being male.[4] When this is combined with the first precept about nonharming, however, the field of reference becomes much wider. Relationships that are harmful or abusive also stand condemned, as are forms of love that seek to possess or imprison another, or to use another only for the gratification of one's own sensual desire. A contemporary set of trainings, devised by the Vietnamese Buddhist monk Thich Nhat Hanh for the lay members of his Order of Interbeing, therefore, includes this:

3. Langenberg, "What Do Buddhists Think?" 322–26.
4. Langenberg, "What Do Buddhists Think?" 323.

Aware that sexual desire is not love and that sexual relations motivated by craving cannot dissipate the feeling of loneliness but will create more suffering, frustration and isolation, we are determined not to engage in sexual relations without mutual understanding, love, and a deep long-term commitment made known to our family and friends. Seeing that body and mind are one, we are committed to learning appropriate ways to take care of our sexual energy and to cultivate loving kindness, compassion, joy and inclusiveness for our own happiness and the happiness of others.[5]

One of the most important early texts about lay relationships within the Pali Canon is the *Sigālaka Sutta*, in which the Buddha is seen conversing with a lay person named Sigālaka, who was carrying out an early morning religious ritual that involved paying homage to the different directions of the earth—the north, the south and so on. The Buddha challenged the young man to move away from dependence on ritual, suggesting that the best way to pay homage to the six directions was through moral action and the avoidance of activities such as drug use, gambling, and idleness. He then told the young man that the right way to protect the six directions was through developing wholesome relationships, after which he matched each direction with a particular relationship. One of these, at the western direction, was between man and wife:

There are five ways in which a husband should minister to his wife as the western direction: by honoring her, by not disparaging her, by not being unfaithful to her, by giving authority to her, by providing her with adornments. And there are five ways in which a wife, thus ministered to by her husband as the western direction, will reciprocate: by properly organizing her work, by being kind to the servants, by not being unfaithful, by protecting stores, and by being skilful and diligent in all she has to do. In this way, the western direction is covered, making it at peace and free from fear.[6]

Although marriage roles are implicitly gendered here, reciprocity between the partners in a marriage is presented as the ideal, together with faithfulness. This continues to be the ideal within Buddhist communities. Marriage partnerships in Buddhist contexts should allow each partner to develop and grow to the extent that it is not unknown in Buddhist

5. "Fourteen Mindfulness Trainings," para. 16.

6. *Sigālaka Sutta*, discourse no. 31 in the *Dīgha Nikāya*, quoted in Walshe, *Long Discourses of the Buddha*, 467.

communities for a married person to renounce and become a monastic if the other partner agrees and is financially secure.

Significant also is that marriage is explicitly linked in the *Sigālaka Sutta* to protecting the world. Other texts implicitly link marriage to protecting societies from harm, immorality, violence and licentiousness. In the reciprocity present in the discourse, the Buddha was a pioneer. His teaching contrasted with the patriarchy present in wider society at the Buddha's time. The Pali Canon contains a book of poems written by the early Buddhist nuns, who left their homes in order to follow the Buddha. Named the *Therīgāthā* (lit.: verses of the women elders), it is one of the earliest global examples of literature written by women. Obvious from these poems is that some of the nuns had experienced abusive marriages, such as the one named Sumangala's mother, who wrote:

> O woman well set free! How free am I,
> How thoroughly free from kitchen drudgery!
> Me stained and squalid 'mong my cooking pots
> My brutal husband ranked as even less
> Than the sunshades he sitting weaves alway.[7]

Affection between partners is not mentioned in the *Sigālaka Sutta* but one could argue for its implicit presence in the reciprocal duties outlined. In other texts it is more explicit. For instance, there is a beautiful narrative in the *Aṅguttara Nikāya* (the Numerical Discourses of the Buddha) of the Pali Canon, in which the Buddha visits the house of a lay couple, who are simply presented as the parents of "Nakula." Both the husband and wife say to the Buddha that they do not recall ever having "transgressed" against each other "in thought, much less by deed," and express a wish to be together in future lives. The implication is that this will either be as humans or in the heavens. The Buddha replies: "Householders, if both husband and wife wish to see one another not only in this present life but also in future lives, they should have the same faith, the same virtuous behaviour, the same generosity, and the same wisdom. Then they will see one another not only in this present life but also in future lives."[8]

In Buddhist cosmology, the heavens are not the final goal of human life but are impermanent states of happiness and bliss that beings can be reborn within as the result of living an exemplary, morally upright life. This

---

7. *Therīgāthā* v. 23, in Rhys Davids, *Poems of the Early Buddhist Nuns*, 19.

8. *Aṅguttara Nikāya*, Book of the Fours, No. 55, in Bodhi, *Numerical Discourses of the Buddha*, 445–46.

text both gives an ideal for marriage partners and hope to the couple concerned that their love for each other will bring them together again. It does not, however, link this with the final goal of Buddhist practice—nirvana. In nirvana, all earthly ties and attachments are broken, including marriage relationships.

Buddhism also speaks of the importance of a good or beautiful friend in one's life—a *kalyaṇa-mitra* in Sanskrit. A good friend is a reliable companion, who can help one practice the Buddhist path. He or she is often a teacher but could also be a spouse. If partners in marriage can also be *kalyaṇa-mitra*s to each other, encouraging each other to develop their generosity, their lovingkindness, and their meditation practice, so much the better.

Marriage, therefore, is not only praised in Buddhism but is also seen as contributing to harmony in society when characterized by an ethic of mutual respect and faithfulness. It is not, however, seen as having divine sanction. As the narrative to which I have just referred implies, Buddhists see marriage as belonging to the mundane and the secular. Buddhist monks and nuns do not officiate at marriage ceremonies, although they are involved in funerals, which have greater religious value in Buddhism. In some Buddhist contexts today, religious verses are sung at weddings, however this is not done by monastics but by lay people. For instance, in Sri Lanka, young women, dressed in white, often sing Buddhist verses in front of the married couple. Influence from Christian religious wedding ceremonies during British rule of the country is one possible explanation for this innovation.

The other great school within Buddhist traditions, Mahayana Buddhism, grew up in India between the first century BCE and the fourth century CE. It developed a new set of holy texts, one of the most well-known of which is *The Lotus Sutra*. This sutra refers to the same fourfold community as the Pali texts. People within all four categories are described as children of the Buddha, who are capable of reaching buddhahood.[9] However,

---

9. There were several differences between Early Buddhism and Mahayana Buddhism. The most fundamental concerned the goal of the Buddhist path. Early Buddhism and contemporary Theravada Buddhism assert that the person who becomes enlightened through hearing the teaching of the Buddha is an *arhat* (worthy one). A Buddha arises when the Buddha's teaching (the Dharma) is not known in the world, after having prepared for this through numerous lives as a buddha-to-be, a *bodhisattva*. Mahayana Buddhism asserted that all beings could become buddhas; all could follow the bodhisattva path.

because the focus of the text is the ultimate goal of Buddhist practice, it contains no specific teaching about marriage, although the institution of marriage is implicit in its illustrations. "Widows and unmarried women," for instance, are mentioned in a negative light as people that one on the path to buddhahood should not associate with![10]

As Buddhism traveled from India, it interacted with and became embedded within a number of different religious cultures. This had an impact on the practice of Buddhism and on its views concerning marriage. For instance, there is evidence that the monastic rule on celibacy was not always adhered to strictly, with some monks remaining in contact with their families. Some nuns even gave birth, with children being cared for in the monastery.[11] This was often hidden from the eyes of laypeople, but in Japan, Buddhist monks eventually became priests rather than monastics and were allowed to marry.

One consequence of the principle of reciprocity within marriage relationships and the fact that marriage was seen as a secular rather than a religious institution was that divorce was not frowned upon in most Buddhist cultures. In addition, women had more rights over the property they brought into the marriage contract than in Western cultures and had greater economic freedom. Sri Lankan historian Lorna Devaraja, for instance, argued that in precolonial Sri Lanka the Sinhala Buddhist legal system allowed for the dissolution of a marriage if either spouse was guilty of improper conduct and that remarriage by either party held no stigma.[12] One source for her argument was the memoir written by Robert Knox (1641–1720), who was held prisoner in the independent Kandyan Kingdom in Sri Lanka between 1669 and 1679.[13] To take another example, Western visitors to Myanmar, when it was under British rule, noted the freedom of Burmese women and the economic responsibilities they held. For instance, R. Talbot Kelly, who traveled throughout the country at the beginning of the twentieth century, after describing the attractive appearance of Burmese women, stated, "In fact, the women seem to monopolise the brain and energy of the race, and occupy an absolutely independent

10. Reeves, *Lotus Sutra*, 264.

11. Collett, "Does Buddhism Have Rules?," 293.

12. E.g., Devaraja, "Position of Women in Buddhism," 118–19.

13. Knox, *Historical Relation*.

position."[14] Traditionally, women in Buddhist cultures were not seen as the property of men, and childbearing was not their only role.

Narratives within the early Buddhist texts, however, also show that marriage did not always live up to the ideal present in the *Sigālakā Sutta* and the example of Nakula's parents. And marriage partners were certainly not always good friends to each other. As disharmony was possible among the communities of monks, so it was possible within lay society, for Buddhism teaches that the eradication of egocentric craving is difficult; our greeds, hatreds and delusions are so deeply embedded within our beings that they can easily get the better of us, resulting in anger, jealousy, and unkindness. One well-known collection of doctrinal verses in the Pali Canon, the *Dhammapada*, has a commentarial narrative attached to each verse, giving the context in which the Buddha taught the verse. Tension and conflict within familial relationships is a recurrent theme in them, both within Buddhist and non-Buddhist families. In one, a husband is embarrassed by his adulterous wife.[15] In another, a wife finds that her husband has been having sexual relations with their slave and punishes the slave mercilessly.[16]

Given that human relationships can go wrong, Buddhism teaches that all relationships, not least marriage, can form the ground within which spiritual progress can be made through the controling and transcending of negative emotions such as anger. Marriage in itself does not constitute a religious practice in Buddhism, but most Buddhists would say the challenges present within it can aid progress along the religious path. Developing the opposites of negative emotions, for instance lovingkindness as an antidote for anger, is one way of transcending the negative within Buddhism. Using meditation in order to know one's mind better is another method of controling negative emotions.

One of the aims of meditation in Buddhism is to know and purify the mind and the emotions. A verse in the *Dhammapada* puts it this way:

> Not to do any evil;
> To undertake what is good;

14. Kelly, *Burma Painted and Described*, 18.

15. This story illustrates verses 242–43 of the *Dhammapada*, the first line of which states "The rust of a woman is misconduct" (Roebuck, *Dhammapada*, 191), "rust" being understood as the "tarnishing" which results from poor actions.

16. This story illustrates verse 314 of the *Dhammapada*: "A bad deed is better not done—You repent a bad deed afterwards. A good deed is better done—One you won't repent when you've done it" (Roebuck, *Dhammapada*, 61 & 203). The story ends with husband, wife, and the slave all becoming followers of the Buddha.

To purify your own mind;
This is the teaching of the Buddhas.[17]

One Buddhist meditative practice helps the meditator to gain insight into what triggers negative emotions that can destroy relationships through watching the mind and feelings, without judging, developing, or owning as mine what arises. In the practice, feelings such as anger arise and are noted but then released. The contemporary mindfulness movement has been influenced by it. One practical fruit of the practice is a developing ability to catch oneself before negative thoughts and emotions are expressed in action, through increased minute-by-minute awareness of what the mind is doing. A Buddhist monk who was one of my teachers of meditation in Sri Lanka said in one session: "Meditation is the ultimate practice of non-violence. Suffering, pain and feelings of anger are not suppressed, but faced, confronted and transformed. To face anger, to recognize and accept it, may mean that it's changed into something like compassion."[18] If Buddhist partners in a marriage relationship are involved in this kind of practice, reconciliation after disputes should be easier and anger less destructive.

Marriage across Religious Traditions

The parents of Nakula are told by the Buddha that they should be united in faith. Does this mean Buddhists are opposed to interreligious marriage? There are no legal restrictions to a Buddhist marrying someone from another religion. Opposition to interreligious marriages has arisen, however, whenever Buddhists have feared that the Buddhist partner would be expected to convert to the other religion or be prevented from carrying out religious observances. One narrative in the commentary to the *Dhammapada* involves just such a situation. Uttarā, a devout Buddhist, is married to a non-Buddhist and is prevented from giving alms to Buddhist monastics. She therefore pays for a beautiful courtesan, Sirimā, to be with her husband while she arranges almsgiving to the monks. Complications arise but Uttarā remains calm and compassionate. Eventually Sirimā becomes a Buddhist, but not the husband.[19]

17. Roebuck, *Dhammapada* v. 183, 36.

18. See Harris, *What Buddhists Believe*, 97.

19. Commentarial story to *Dhammapada* verse 223: "By freedom from anger you should conquer anger,/By good conquer what is not good,/By giving conquer miserliness,/By truth the teller of lies" (Roebuck, *Dhammapada*, 44, 187).

The evidence of the Pali Canon suggests the context of philosophical debate within which Buddhism arose could become acrimonious, as different religious groupings disagreed over philosophical issues and also competed for alms from lay people. Although some early Buddhist texts ridiculed or subordinated beliefs held by other religious groups, the Buddha seems to have promoted an attitude that combined respect with reasoned debate. In one early text, the Buddha is seen giving this advice to his monastic followers if someone from another group ridiculed his teaching:

> Monks, if anyone should speak in disparagement of me, of the Dhamma or of the Sangha, you should not be angry, resentful or upset on that account. If you were to be angry or displeased at such disparagement, that would only be a hindrance to you . . . If others disparage me, the Dhamma or the Sangha, then you must explain what is incorrect, as being incorrect, saying: "That is incorrect, that is false, that is not our way, that is not found among us."[20]

Within early Buddhist responses to religious others, there was, however, a tension between the Buddha's teaching that one should not cling to one's identity and one's views, and the conviction among his followers that the wisdom of the Buddha was superior to the teachings present in other religious traditions because of teachings such as this.[21] In the centuries following the Buddha's death, conflict arose with the brahmanical tradition[22] and, during periods of Western mission and expansionism, with Christianity. Japan, for instance, proscribed Christianity at the beginning of the seventeenth century because of the missionary activities of the Jesuits; only in the 1870s was this reversed.[23] In Sri Lanka and Myanmar, the activities of British and American evangelical missionaries under British colonial rule were aggressively countered by Buddhists in revivalist movements that were predicated on opposition to Christianity.[24] In the present, there is conflict with Muslims in several Buddhist-majority countries. Generally, however, Buddhists have preferred respectful co-existence with other religious traditions rather than polemics. When courtesy has been shown to Buddhism, courtesy has always been returned. And on the contrary, when

20. *Brahmajāla Sutta*, discourse No. 1 in the *Digha Nikaya*, in Walshe, *Long Discourses of the Buddha*, 68.

21. Harris, "Buddhism and the Religious Other," 92.

22. Schmidt-Leukel, "Buddhist-Hindu Relations."

23. Harris, "Buddhism and the Religious Other," 100–104.

24. Harris, *Theravāda Buddhism*, 191–204.

a threat to Buddhism has been seen through the action of people within other religions, defensive and hostile action has been taken.

Similar principles apply in the context of interreligious marriage. In postcolonial countries in Asia—such as Cambodia, Myanmar, and Sri Lanka, where mistrust remains between Buddhists and Christians, and indeed Buddhists and Muslims—interreligious marriages can be vigorously opposed because of the fear that the Buddhist partner will be forced to convert to the other religion and will not be affirmed in his or her faith. They, nevertheless, occur and often succeed, particularly when both partners respect each other's beliefs and practice. Formal interreligious dialogue in these countries in the twentieth and twenty-first centuries has also helped to modify the fears of Buddhists in this area.

In the West, interreligious dialogue has brought Western and Asian Buddhists together with people of other religions, creating an environment in which Buddhists are comfortable with interreligious marriages if, again, they are characterized by mutual respect and mutual affirmation of the two faiths concerned. Yet, it must be added that a sizeable number of Western Buddhists converted to Buddhism from Judaism or Christianity and some of these are unwilling to have much to do with their former faiths, even when asked to engage in interreligious dialogue.

Concluding Thoughts

I have argued for the centrality of marriage within Buddhist lay societies. The Buddhist ideal of marriage is that it should be characterized by mutual respect and reciprocity. This ideal has given considerable independence to women in Buddhist contexts. Because of the secular nature of marriage in Buddhism, there are no religious strictures against interreligious marriage. However, religious considerations enter if the Buddhist partner within such a marriage is prevented from practicing Buddhism and, therefore, progressing spiritually. Particularly in postcolonial situations, fear concerning this is still rife. However, where there is mutual respect between partners and affirmation of both of the religions present in the marriage, then interreligious marriages can be celebrated with joy in Buddhist contexts.

CHAPTER 13

Human Purpose and Marriage in Zoroastrianism

ONE OF THE WORLD's oldest religious faiths is also one of the least known today. Zoroastrianism is built of the teachings of Zarathushtra, an Iranian priest-prophet who lived around 1200 BCE and who received revelations proclaiming Ahura Mazda as the Great Creator. At the height of its influence around 550 BC, Zoroastrianism was the religion of the greatest empire of the ancient world, that of Persia (modern-day Iran), led by Cyrus the Great. Perhaps the first monotheistic faith tradition, Zoroastrianism first developed the concepts of God as Creator, Heaven and Hell, and resurrection from the dead. These spread to other religions as Zoroastrians came into contact with Jews, Christians, Muslims, Buddhists, and Hindus. Some of these interactions with other faiths also brought deep persecution, which prompted Zoroastrianism to keep its practices and theology secret, so that many of its own descendants, nearly all of whom now live outside of Iran, know little of it today.

The ancient ancestors of the Zoroastrians were proto-Indo-Iranian tribes who migrated from the steppes of Asia into what is today Eastern Iran around the end of the second millennium BC.[1] Some of their counterparts moved into India where the Brahmin form of Hinduism developed; several similarities between Hinduism and Zoroastrianism still exist, though distinct differences have also evolved. Zarathushtra himself was a historical figure born into this social milieu at a time of political conflict,

---

1. Boyce, *Textual Sources*, 6–7.

war, and social upheaval. The divine inspirations he received around age thirty, along with his personal feeling of physical helplessness, convinced him of the importance of justice and morality in all areas of life from the personal to the communal, from the religious to the political.[2] Zarathushtra became particularly convinced of the cosmic struggle between good and evil and that human as well as divine beings had an important part to play in the battles. Good thoughts, good words, good actions were the responsibility and sacrifice required of humans.

Zarathushtra's revelations were passed down orally for many centuries, especially in the form of seventeen hymns, known as the *Gathas*. These reveal his understanding and worship of Ahura Mazda (later known as Ormazd) as the one God who created all in his munificence. Zarathushtra also composed a prayer praising Ahura Mazda called the *Ahuna Vairya,* which served a similar function for his followers as the Lord's Prayer does for Christians. He extended an existing practice of prayer three times a day (morning, noon, and night) to five times daily. Zarathushtra instituted seven high feasts spread across the year which focused on different elements of creation and inculcated a sense of communal belonging, discipline, and doctrinal affirmations among the faithful.[3]

Zarathushtra's monotheistic affirmation of one God was accompanied by a dualistic understanding of an ongoing battle between good and evil. Ahura Mazda, the ultimately triumphant Creator God, was pitted against Angra Mainyu (also known as Ahriman), the Hostile Spirit. This duel between good and evil, darkness and light, life and death, was not only fought by divine bodies but necessarily engaged humans as well. Zarathushtra was the first known priest/prophet to teach of the individual's responsibility to choose between good and evil.[4] He contradicted the existing belief which stated that only kings or priests could go to heaven and all commoners, women, and children would go to hell; in Zarathushtra's understanding, the afterlife of each was based on their deeds rather than their social status. While this teaching angered many people in high places, it followed logically from Zarathushtra's deep faith in justice and the rule of law. It also introduced a certain egalitarianism into society and deepened the responsibility of the individual to think and speak and act for justice on behalf of all persons and all of creation.

2. Boyce, *Zoroastrians*, 19.

3. Boyce, *Zoroastrians*, 32–33.

4. Boyce, *Zoroastrians*, 29.

The individual's responsibility to act for good is a crucial part of the Zoroastrian creation stories which describe history/time as being a finite period of some 12,000 years.[5] According to this concept, "thought"—known as *menog* and representing the spiritual aspects of creation—existed before the material world of *getig*, or "creation with bones," came to be. In the dualistic understanding, the *menog* was the "mother" while the *getig* was the "father."[6] The concepts of good and evil are also expressed as *asha* and *drug*, with *asha* standing for truth, honesty, loyalty, and courage, and *drug* representing that which is untrue, unreal, crooked, devious.[7] *Asha* is that which brings "order" in the physical world, and "righteousness" in the ethical sphere. At the end of time, *asha* will "have bones,"[8] and all will live in peace.[9]

Creation

In the Zoroastrian creation story, seven elements appeared in stages: sky, water, earth, a single plant, a bull, a man, and fire.[10] All these were then combined under the fire (sun) in the sky, when the gods sacrificed a single plant, a bull, and a man to set in motion all the rest of creation. These original elements came to be recognized as lesser deities; the six of them, along with Ahura Mazda, were known collectively as the Heptad (the Seven).[11] In turn the Heptad became associated with divine attributes: Good Thought, Best Order, Well-deserved Command, Life-giving Humility, Wholeness, and Undyingness (not dying before one's time). In the Zoroastrian understanding, the Heptad was not a polytheistic rendering of many gods so much as a monotheistic personification of divine attributes to be worshiped. It transforms the concept of "God is love" into "Love is god."[12] These lesser deities have *spenta* (holiness, power to aid),[13] all of which are needed

---

5. Skjaervo, *Spirit of Zoroastrianism*, 1; Rose, *Zoroastrianism*, 109–10.

6. Boyce, *Textual Sources*, 48.

7. Boyce, *Zoroastrians*, 8; Skjaervo, *Spirit of Zoroastrianism*, 11.

8. Skjaervo, *Spirit of Zoroastrianism* 11.

9. Boyce, *Zoroastrians*, 26.

10. Boyce, *Textual Sources*, 10.

11. Boyce, *Textual Sources*, 12.

12. Boyce, *Zoroastrians*, 10.

13. Boyce, *Zoroastrians*, 24.

for victory of good over evil.[14] In the ritual world, the priest (human) symbolically combines butter, milk, a sacred plant, water, and fire on earth to represent the original sacrifice of creation. It is significant that though all the divine elements are necessary for this ritual (and its subsequent impact on all creation), the ultimate responsibility for the victory of good over evil in creation lies with humans. Along with that responsibility for ritual also comes the responsibility for goodness in one's person as seen in the necessity for the priest to ensure that he maintains good thoughts, good words, and good actions in order for the sacrifice to be acceptable.[15]

This human responsibility for goodness permeates all aspects of a Zoroastrian's life. Whether making land productive by sowing seeds, irrigating, or draining swamp land, giving fodder to cattle or carrying wood to fire: any action that would reenergize creation is a good deed. Good deeds are also to be done to the vulnerable of society, especially helping the poor and participating in philanthropy. Deeds of justice are better than those done merely for oneself.[16]

The good deeds of humans emanate from good thoughts, and so daily prayers are essential for Zoroastrians. Good deeds, good words, and good thoughts are also all intimately integrated in the *Navjote* (new birth) initiation ceremony, which each Zoroastrian can undertake between the age of seven and fifteen. In the *Navjote*, the individual takes his or her rightful place in the community and assumes responsibility for his or her own thoughts, words, and actions. Two items of clothing are received in the *Navjote*: a white woven cotton undershirt called a *sudreh*, and a wool cord worn around the waist called a *kusti*. The *sudreh* has a small pocket in front

14. Skjaervo, *Spirit of Zoroastrianism*, 14.

15. Rose, *Zoroastrianism*,167: A reverence for both water and fire existed in the pre-Zoroastrianism religious cults and developed into the tradition of keeping a hearth-fire ever-burning in the home. According to Boyce, *Textual Sources*, 61, this symbol of the preservation of justice and *asha* evolved into the Zoroastrian fire-temples which centralized and symbolized the might and strength of priests and rulers. While the priests for the fire-temples could only be male, caring for water, especially in the sense of keeping it free from pollution and offering it as a libation, was especially a duty for women.

16. Boyce, *Textual Sources*, 100; Rose, *Zoroastrianism*, 26, 44, 75, 118. The concepts of good and evil also assigned to objects: dogs, birds, and hedgehogs (for example) were considered good, while others, such as water rats or toads, were considered evil. Because evil objects polluted rather than purified, they should be destroyed. Since water, fire, and the earth could purify or be polluted, and dead bodies were considered polluting, disposal of corpses presented a special challenge. This led to the still-prevalent practice amongst Zoroastrians of leaving dead bodies exposed to the elements (usually in Towers of Silence) rather than pollute the earth or fire by burial or cremation.

in which good deeds can be symbolically accumulated; the *kusti* winds around the waist as a barrier against evil, a kind of cosmic girdle.[17] The *kusti* is to be untied and retied several times a day in response to polluting influences of bodily functions; after washing, the wearer prays to Ahura Mazda, holding the untied ends of the *kusti* (facing fire, if possible), then curses Angra Mainyu (the devil) by flicking the ends of the cords menacingly, then retying the cords while still praying.[18] The repeated ritual of tying the *kusti* becomes a constant act of personal involvement with the cosmic world, reminding the observant Zoroastrian of their responsibility, through good thoughts, words, and actions, to maintain equilibrium between good and evil in the universe.

Creation of Humans

While there is no specific description of the creation of humans in the *Avesta*, humans are prominent in the Zoroastrian creation story, created alongside the "single plant" and the Bull (representing all animals).[19] The original human was known as Gayomard, a figure similar to Adam of the Genesis story, especially in that he was "good." In a catechism called "Selected Precepts of the Ancient Sages," a follower of Zoroaster can claim:

> . . . I belong to Ohrmazd, not to Ahriman . . . to the good, not to the bad. My stock and lineage is from Gayomard. My mother is Spendarmad, my father Ohrmazd, my humanity is from Mahre and Mahryane, who were the first off-spring and seed of Gayomard.[20]

This latter reference is to a Zoroastrian understanding that when the original single person, plant, and bull were comingled, six pairs of twins emerged, each set consisting of one male and one female. These twins then married each other so that a further fifteen pairs of twins were produced, all of whom intermarried again, leading eventually to a full population.[21] While this creation story, perhaps innocently enough, ignores the near-universal incest taboo, it upholds a theology of sustaining goodness in terms of purity by encouraging an adherence to one's own kind, which is

17. Rose, *Zoroastrianism*, 26; Skjaervo, *Spirit of Zoroastrianism*, 34.

18. Boyce, *Zoroastrians*, 33.

19. Skjaervo, *Spirit of Zoroastrianism*, 21.

20. Cited in Boyce, *Textual Sources*, 99.

21. Greater Bundahishn, ch. 14, quoted in Boyce, *Textual Sources*, 52.

especially deemed essential in times of conflict with competing religious tribes and cultural groups. Indeed, the Zoroastrian tradition of intermarriage *khvaetvadatha* or *khvedodah*—"next-of-kin marriage"[22]—still exists in some conservative circles where marrying one's first cousin is considered a favorable arrangement.

Gender Roles

As with nearly all ancient faith traditions, the male is considered the normative human in Zoroastrianism, though women are specifically included in the sacred texts, even though those texts were probably exclusively composed, translated, and interpreted by males.[23] The Zoroastrian priesthood remains an exclusively male position of *mobads* or *magi*, but there are also provisions that permit any man, woman, or child who could recite the ritual (*zasthra*) by heart to perform a ritual.[24] Both men and women go to the fire temple for worship in the same way.[25] A daughter could also inherit responsibility for the family hearth-fire from her father, but at the time of her marriage, she would be required to turn that priestly function over to her husband's care.[26]

During the Sasanian period, the last of the great flourishing of Zoroastrianism in Iran before the Muslim conquest, there are some accounts of upper-class women managing family estates.[27] Still, the traditional roles for women were primarily in the domestic sphere: educating children, preparing for ritual, social welfare. The female goddess, *Ashii* (reward), was called upon to bless dwellings. A hymn to Ashii speaks of "couches . . . well-spread, well perfumed, well fashioned, provided with cushions . . . [at which] wives assuredly sit expectantly . . . waiting . . . for 'the master of the dwelling' to arrive."[28]

One of the traditional daily rituals for a woman in the home is known as *laban*; in this she spreads the fragrance of incense throughout the house.

22. Boyce, *Zoroastrians*, xxi.

23. Rose, *Zoroastrianism*, 5.

24. Neragestar, 30, quoted in Rose, *Zoroastrianism*, 84. Interesting that the word *mobad/magi* became the word for 'magic' in Greek.

25. Boyce, *Textual Sources*, 145.

26. Rose, *Zoroastrianism*, 118.

27. From *The Book of a Thousand Legal Decisions* cited in Rose, *Zoroastrianism*, 118.

28. Boyce, *Textual Sources*, 31.

As with other Zoroastrian rituals, the *laban* also symbolizes the spreading of goodness all around. A contemporary Zoroastrian woman practicing *laban* reflects, "Similarly I promise to lead a useful life filled with good deeds that will leave a memorable mark on the world."[29]

Marriage

Within the Zoroastrian understanding of the goodness of creation, the physical, that is, the sexual, side of marriage is considered good. While there is little explicit eroticism in the Zoroastrian scriptures, procreation is praised as a primary purpose of marriage. Indeed, according to the catechism referred to above, a Zoroastrian's second most important duty is to "take a wife and beget earthly progeny. He should be diligent in this and not neglectful of it."[30] The catechism continues to advise that educating these offspring is also an essential responsibility that lies with both the father and the mother; by the time the offspring are fifteen years old, they should know their duties and how to perform them. The catechism also states that the parents are responsible for the sins of the child, even after the child's maturity.

The Zoroastrian scriptures also have little to say about the role of spirituality in marriage or the role of marriage in developing spirituality, but some clues can be teased from the epic romantic poem, *Vis and Ramin,* written in the eleventh century by the Persian poet, Fakhraddin Gorgani. The lengthy poem (nearly 500 pages in English translation) harkens back to an earlier Iranian age with an effusive tale of romance, love, morality, and eroticism involving a Persian princess, Vis, and the three men who become her husbands.

Most startling about this story (for non-Zoroastrians) is the somewhat nonchalant acceptance of the tradition of next-of-kin marriage: Vis's first husband is her brother, Viru; her second and third husbands are brothers of each other. Yet the characters (and the narrator) of the story are more concerned that Vis is in an adulterous relationship with Ramin (her third husband) while still married to her second husband, King Mobad. Early on, the reader is hostile toward Mobad for attempting to seduce Vis's mother (before Vis is born); she rebuffs him with the promise that he can wed her

---

29. Rose, *Zoroastrianism,* 6.

30. From "*Selected Precepts of the Ancient Sages: a brief catechism,*" 9.1.1, cited in Boyce, *Textual Sources,* 100.

yet-to-be-conceived daughter. As the story progresses, Mobad emerges as a violent and vindictive tyrant, as well as an abusive husband to Vis, so the reader sees her adultery in a more sympathetic light. Much is made of the love between Vis and Ramin (though Vis also loves her husband-brother Viru). The story also makes clear that neither Vis's marriage to Viru or King Mobad was consummated and so gives credence to her relationship with Ramin.

Ultimately, the story portrays a strong-willed and passionate woman who rails against hierarchy, child marriage, and blind allegiance to oaths. In the story, Vis is faithful to the goodness of love rather than social obligation. The fact that her name is first in the title of the story points to her right to be respected: her female desires and feelings are to be honored as much as the king's, even though he retains significantly more physical, legal, and economic power.

After Mobad's death, Vis and Ramin are finally free to marry, and peace reigns throughout the land, not least because as Ramin becomes king in place of his brother he "handed all his kingship to his queen [Vis] who governed both the world now and Ramin."[31] Their union produces two sons and a kingdom ruled with justice and harmony.[32] The female becomes a heroine because of her domestic and political as well as procreative competency.

Interfaith Relations

A faith tradition which has prized next-of-kin marriage certainly struggles with the contemporary concept of interfaith marriage. As noted above, purity (assumed through keeping to one's own tribe/family group) was not only linked with goodness but probably linked to a long history of interfaith conflicts in which Zoroastrians often found themselves being persecuted. Though historical clashes with Jews, Christians, and Manichaeans had turned violent at times, the Muslim conquest at Merv in Iran in 651 CE brought the end to the golden age of Zoroastrianism.[33] Muslims, being people of a book, particularly considered Zoroastrianism inferior at this time because it had no written text, having relied solely on oral transmission of

---

31. Gorgani, *Vis and Ramin*, 492.

32. Rose, *Zoroastrianism*, 77.

33. Rose, *Zoroastrianism*, xxii.

its scriptures from ancient times.[34] Both religions, even when attempting to co-exist in Iran, considered the other ritually polluting, so there were restrictions about what facilities members those of each faith community could use, like bath houses, for instance. Still, at least initially under Islamic rule, the Zoroastrians were considered a protected minority though they had to pay a tax for the privilege. Interfaith marriage could only take place if the Zoroastrian spouse converted to Islam.[35]

As the Zoroastrian situation in Iran under Muslim rule gradually became more intolerable, a large group of Zoroastrians left Iran for India between the mid-seventh and early-tenth centuries.[36] Known as Parsis, the immigrants found a much warmer welcome from the Hindus in India, perhaps because of several similarities between Hinduism and Zoroastrianism, including a reverence for the sun, moon, water, fire, and cows, and the wearing of a sacred girdle. While the Zoroastrian newcomers were welcomed to India, there were restrictions imposed on them: they had to abandon their Iranian language and all weapons; the women had to wear Indian dress; they were forbidden to proselytize; and their marriages had to take place at night. Eventually the Parsis centralized their presence in Mumbai, where they became highly regarded for their skills in commerce.

While the Parsis have flourished commercially over the centuries, their numbers have diminished, partly because transmission of the faith traditions suffered as education of priests was neglected, which resulted in a dire shortage of religious leaders. The decrease in Parsi population has also been attributed to low birth rates and interfaith marriages, as it was mandated in 1908 that one must have a Parsi father to be considered Parsi.[37] As adherence to Zoroastrianism and its numbers have decreased, there has been a more general acceptance of interfaith marriage. The reality of this situation was recognized in part in 2005 when a meeting hall was opened in Mumbai which allowed for public navjotes and interfaith marriage ceremonies.[38] Within many of those contemporary interfaith mar-

34. Rose, *Zoroastrianism*, 104. In fact, the Zoroastrians had no written alphabet for their sacred ancient Avesta language until the sixth/seventh centuries CE. That date corresponds with the subsequent development of the Avestan alphabet, probably a Zoroastrian response to the persecution meted out by the Muslims.

35. Rose, *Zoroastrianism*, 181.

36. Rose, *Zoroastrianism*, 190.

37. Boyce, *Textual Sources*, 153. Conversion to Zoroastrianism is allowed but does not make one a Parsi.

38. Rose, *Zoroastrianism*, 211.

riages, a desire to better know and understand Zoroastrianism burns, akin to the ever-burning hearth-fires of the ancient faith traditions.

Summary

A Zoroastrian's duty and purpose in life is to maintain a positive equilibrium in the cosmos through his or her good thoughts, good words, and good actions. While there are some restrictions as to which actions can be done by males or females, the responsibility for goodness is the same for both sexes.

Zoroastrians consider physical intimacy to be part of the goodness of creation, so begetting a child is considered one of the good responsibilities of an adult (male), and sexual relations within marriage are considered good and healthy.

Endogamous marriage, that is, within one's immediate family, has traditionally been preferred within Zoroastrianism, perhaps in part because of the faith tradition's long experience of conflict and conquest with outside groups. Still, interfaith marriage today has become more common, and the Zoroastrian community has taken steps to widen its understanding of how a tiny faith tradition can survive in the contemporary world.

CHAPTER 14

Marriage and the Bahá'í Faith

BY DAVID GRANT AND WENDI MOMEN

THE BAHÁ'Í FAITH is an independent world religion. The fundamental principles enunciated by Bahá'u'lláh (1817–92), the Prophet-Founder of the Bahá'í faith, are that there is one God, that there is only one religion— progressively revealed to humanity by a succession of great teachers known as Manifestations or Messengers—and that there is one human family:

> In thousands upon thousands of locations around the world, the teachings of the Bahá'í Faith inspire individuals and communities as they work to improve their own lives and contribute to the advancement of civilization. Bahá'í teachings address such essential themes as the inherent nobility of the human being; the development of spiritual qualities; freedom from all forms of prejudice, the integration of worship and service; the equality of women and men; the harmony of the two great systems of knowledge, religion and science; the centrality of justice to all human endeavours; the importance of education, and the dynamics of the relationships that are to bind together individuals, communities and institutions as humanity advances toward its collective maturity.[1]

These principles not only underpin the religion itself but are fundamental to understanding how Bahá'ís perceive the role and purpose of marriage in the establishment of an ever-advancing civilization.

1. 'What Bahá'ís Believe,' para. 1.

Bahá'u'lláh's message to the world enables the carrying forward of an ever-advancing civilization.[2] His teachings, in the middle of the nineteenth century, came at a time when many parts of the world were in turmoil and dominated by powerful, dark forces. Most countries and territories of the world were now known at this time, and the need for all people, regardless of their faith, culture, or background, to unite to bring peace to the world was more important than ever. Bahá'ís strive to develop and acquire positive virtues in the belief that Bahá'u'lláh's teachings will unite the world and bring all faiths together. While much progress has been made in recent years regarding material progress around the world, Bahá'ís believe that the current materialistic, pleasure-oriented, unjust, poverty-ridden, cruel, wartorn, and excessive society we see today is not the sort of civilization envisaged by Bahá'u'lláh. It is accepted, however, that many elements of today's society are beautiful, cultured, useful, noble, and worth carrying forward. What is missing is a much greater emphasis on the spiritual dimensions of society, which provides dignity to humanity and confers true joys as well as material well-being. Bahá'u'lláh diagnosed the illness of the world community as disunity among its people. The remedy, he stated, is to establish that unity at every level, from the family to the global.

As the Torah is to Jews, the Bible to Christians, or the Qur'an to Muslims, the collected writings of Bahá'u'lláh are considered by Bahá'ís to be revelation from God. These writings form the foundation of the Bahá'í faith and provide the guidance essential for the united, loving, and spiritually enlightened marriages and families that form the bedrock of communities and nations that support a similarly united, loving, spiritually enlightened, peaceful, just, and sustainable world.

God's Purpose for Humanity

All Bahá'ís believe the purpose of human life is to know and love God, and by doing so, to acquire virtues and spiritual qualities that enable them to carry forward an ever-advancing civilization. Bahá'ís view life in this world as a preparation for life in the next. The soul comes into existence at conception and is immortal. The nature, purpose, and practice of Bahá'í marriage is embedded within these values. Bahá'u'lláh has said, "The purpose

2. Bahá'u'lláh, *Gleanings, no. 109.*

of God in creating man hath been, and ever will be, to enable him to know his Creator and to attain His Presence,"[3] and:

> Having created the world and all that liveth and moveth therein, He, through the direct operation of His unconstrained and sovereign Will, chose to confer upon man the unique distinction and capacity to know Him and to love Him—a capacity that must needs be regarded as the generating impulse and the primary purpose underlying the whole of creation.[4]

Bahá'í Marriage

The fundamental importance of unity to Bahá'ís cannot be overestimated. Marriage is a physical and spiritual union, an attachment of minds and hearts. In a true Bahá'í marriage, the couple strive to become fully united so their union may continue eternally.[5]

So important is unity for the survival and progress of the world that every human relationship is predicated upon it. Thus Bahá'u'lláh encouraged his followers to marry as an "assistance" to themselves and described marriage as a "fortress for well-being and salvation."[6] For Bahá'ís, marriage is the commitment of a man and a woman to each other and is based on love, trust, loyalty, and faithfulness. Without such commitment and faithfulness, the very basis of the higher unities of community, nation, and the world are weakened and jeopardized. In keeping with the imperative of unity, Bahá'u'lláh requires that prospective marriage partners of whatever age seek the permission of their parents before marrying, thereby ensuring that the union of the marriage partners also becomes a union of families, thus establishing a strong bond at the very base of the pyramid of society.

The unity of husband and wife transcends their physical life together, if they have established spiritual bonds, and continues after their death. Marriage partners are to help each other improve their spiritual lives and create the conditions and environment within their marriage that enables each to contribute to the wider world.

---

3. Bahá'u'lláh, *Gleanings, no. 29*.
4. Bahá'u'lláh, *Gleanings, no. 27*.
5. 'Abdu'l-Bahá, *Selections*, 117–18.
6. *Bahá'í Prayers*, 105.

A foundational principle of Bahá'í marriage is the equality of women and men. The implications of this principle reach far beyond the home into the community, the workplace, and eventually into international relations. Far from being a maxim that merely helps a couple determine who does what tasks in the family setting, this basic teaching of the Bahá'í faith is a driver of all the attitudes, behaviors, and practices of the marriage partners in relationship to each other, to their children, and to everyone else.

The Bahá'í Home and Family Life

My home is the home of peace. My home is the home of joy and delight. My home is the home of laughter and exultation. Who-soever enters through the portals of this home, must go out with gladsome heart. This is the home of light; whosoever enters here must become illumined.[7]

This quote comes from the son of Bahá'u'lláh, 'Abdu'l-Bahá, who was imprisoned for forty years. Nevertheless, he provides a vision of a home as the nexus of all the elements of the spiritual, physical, emotional, intellectual, educational and nurturing life of the individual, family, and community. This typifies the Bahá'í approach to the interconnectedness of all aspects of the religion and of life itself. The role of the home and homemakers, both female and male, and of the family is central to the Bahá'í understanding of the purpose of life at the personal level and in the wider community. The home depicted here is peaceful and contributes to peace in society. It is happy and endows others with that happiness. It is a place where true education of the mind and the soul occurs, and where the people who live in it and everyone who encounters it gains in wisdom and grows spiritually. There is energy, a zest for life itself, in such a home, and living there is exhilarating.

The Bahá'í home is the focus of many of the activities associated with Bahá'í community life, including devotional gatherings, meetings where inquirers can learn about the religion, and children's classes. Bahá'ís are urged to invite people of all backgrounds into their homes, and the offering of hospitality in one's home is a significant aspect of Bahá'í life.

7. Abdu'l-Bahá, "My Home," 40. It is interesting to note that 'Abdu'l-Bahá was describing his own home, in which he was a prisoner of the Ottoman Turks from 1868 until 1908.

The Bahá'í home is at once the foundation of and the model for the unified world society envisioned by Bahá'u'lláh. It provides the seedbed and training ground for people who will foster unity at every level of society and who will know how to live in, participate in, and govern such unified communities. The impetus toward unity is acknowledged by Bahá'ís as the imperative of the present human condition and the unity of humanity is the overarching thrust of the teachings of Bahá'u'lláh. It is not surprising, then, that the unity of the home and the family, which forms the basic unit of society, is taken so seriously by Bahá'ís and that they strive to embed within their homes and families the ethical values, attitudes, behaviors, and practices that will inevitably be taken into the workplace, the community, and ultimately into the international arena.

Family life is the bedrock of the whole structure of human society. This includes the procreation and education of children, but it is for the couple of decide if and when they will have children. Bahá'u'lláh encourages the procreation of children: "He that bringeth up his son or the son of another, it is as though he hath brought up a son of Mine."[8] This also means that couples who are unable to have children are free to foster or adopt if they wish. There are no direct references in the Bahá'í texts regarding birth control but the international governing council of the Bahá'í faith, the Universal House of Justice, has stated that although a primary purpose of marriage is the procreation of children, this "does not imply that a couple are obliged to have as many children as they can"; it is "for the husband and wife to decide how many children they would have."[9] Abortion to prevent the birth of an unwanted child is strictly forbidden, though in other circumstances, medical advice should be sought.[10]

A family must be taught all the Bahá'í virtues and that each family member has both rights—which are not to be transgressed—and obligations to other family members.[11] The values that are the building blocks of the Bahá'í home and family are the same as those needed at every level of the Bahá'í community: love, fidelity, justice, honesty, trustworthiness, integrity, the equality of women and men, honoring the intellect, and holding

8. Bahá'u'lláh, *Kitáb-i-Aqdas*, para. 48. The use of the male pronoun is taken to mean either male or female.

9. The Universal House of Justice, "Letter to an Individual 28 January, 1977."

10. Universal House of Justice, in *Lights of Guidance*, 344–47.

11. 'Abdu'l-Bahá, *Promulgation of Universal Peace*, 168.

spiritual purity and detachment in high regard. The education of children is a responsibility of both parents and of the community at large.

The Bahá'í family is considered both the foundation of and the model for the unified world society envisioned by Bahá'u'lláh:

> Compare the nations of the world to the members of a family. A family is a nation in miniature. Simply enlarge the circle of the household, and you have the nation. Enlarge the circle of nations, and you have all humanity. The conditions surrounding the family surround the nation. The happenings in the family are the happenings in the life of the nation. Would it add to the progress and advancement of a family if dissensions should arise among its members, all fighting, pillaging each other, jealous and revengeful of injury, seeking selfish advantage? Nay, this would be the cause of the effacement of progress and advancement. So it is in the great family of nations, for nations are but an aggregate of families. Therefore, as strife and dissension destroy a family and prevent its progress, so nations are destroyed and advancement hindered.[12]

Bahá'í Marriage Laws and Requirements

A Bahá'í marriage is a union between consenting adults: a man and a woman.[13] Marriage is considered a physical and spiritual union, borne out of love for one another, trust, loyalty, and faithfulness. The wedding is the start of a journey for the couple's life together. Marriage and weddings are part of the same process of building civilization and are not just physical relationships that end at death.

Marriage is highly recommended but not obligatory. Bahá'ís are free to marry whom they choose, regardless of the other person's religion or belief (or lack thereof). The consent of all living, natural parents of both parties is required for any Bahá'í wishing to marry, so that unity is created between the two families. The Bahá'ís cannot promise to bring the child up in another religion if their partner is of another faith. The couple must first become acquainted with one another; arranged or forced marriages and plurality of spouses are forbidden, and couples are required to practice

---

12. Abdu'l-Bahá, *Promulgation of Universal Peace*, 157.

13. For further information, see https://www.bahai.org/beliefs/life-spirit/character -conduct/articles-resources/compilation-family-life-marriage.

chastity before marriage and be faithful during marriage. Loyalty to one's marriage partner is a key virtue:

> Chastity implies both before and after marriage an unsullied, chaste sex life. Before marriage absolutely chaste, after marriage absolutely faithful to one's chosen companion. Faithful in all sexual acts, faithful in word and in deed. Chastity is "highly commendable ethically" and is the "only way to a happy and successful marital life."[14]

The conventional practice of a man proposing marriage to a woman is altered in the Bahá'í faith, enabling a woman to propose marriage to a man if they wish. This reflects the fundamental principle of equality of women and men. A period of engagement follows and is expected to be as short as possible. For Iranian Bahá'ís marrying other Iranian Bahá'ís, the engagement period must not exceed ninety-five days.

Bahá'í weddings have only one requirement: the exchange of wedding vows by the marriage partners who state in turn: "We will all, verily, abide by the Will of God."[15] The vows are made in the presence of two witnesses and a Bahá'í Local or National Spiritual Assembly. No one performs the Bahá'í ceremony, as a member of the clergy might do in another religion. The role of the Bahá'í Local or National Spiritual Assembly is to ensure that the various requirements of Bahá'í law (e.g., obtaining the consent of parents) are met. Beyond these basic requirements, the couple are free to choose prayers and readings from Bahá'í scriptures, music, poetry, or other elements as they wish. The ceremony does not require the exchange of rings or other tokens; this is a matter for the couple to decide.

Divorce is allowed but is discouraged. Should a Bahá'í couple feel that their relationship has broken down, marriage partners are encouraged to pray and meditate, to study the Bahá'í texts on marriage, unity, and consultation, and to consult together. Should this not resolve their differences, they are required to undertake a year of patience to make every effort to reconcile any differences. Support is available for the couple during this period. It is hoped that this will enable the couple to continue with their marriage. If this is not successful, then the divorce can take place. Once divorced, Bahá'ís are free to remarry if they wish.

14. Universal House of Justice, *Messages 1963–1986*, 233; and Momen with Momen, *Understanding the Bahá'í Faith*. Same-sex marriages are not permitted in the Bahá'í faith.

15. Bahá'u'lláh, in *Bahá'í Prayers*, 104.

The legal status of Bahá'í marriage varies around the world. In the UK, Bahá'í marriage ceremonies in both Scotland and Northern Ireland are legal if performed by a Bahá'í marriage officer, who is appointed by the National Spiritual Assembly. They oversee the Bahá'í wedding and undertake the legal requirements usually provided by an authorized civil wedding celebrant, which means that a second ceremony (either civil, or in a place of worship if one of the couple is not a Bahá'í) is not required. In England and Wales, the Bahá'í wedding and the registrar wedding need to take place in the same twenty-four-hour period, with no intervening night, so, effectively, on the same day. It does not matter which comes first.

Interfaith Marriage and the Bahá'í Faith

As Bahá'ís are free to marry anyone they choose, whether Bahá'í or not, it is a feature of the Bahá'í community that there are many marriages across ethnic, cultural, social, racial, national, and religious heritages. The Bahá'í community is well endowed with families of mixed parentage going back many generations and is familiar with the challenges this may bring to individuals, families, and communities. It is characteristic of Bahá'ís that they revel in such diversity and often actively encourage their children to seek marriage partners from a different background. A Bahá'í marrying a person of another religion is to be respectful of their partner's beliefs and practices, recalling that, for a Bahá'í, the basis of every religion is the same.

Bahá'ís who marry a person of another religion may be married in the holy place (e.g., church, temple, synagogue, mosque) of the other party, providing a Bahá'í ceremony can also be held there at the same time, or the Bahá'í ceremony can be held elsewhere on the same day. A Bahá'í marrying another Bahá'í should not use the holy place of another religion for their ceremony. A Bahá'í marrying someone from another faith (or no faith) still requires consent of all living parents; this is an essential part of the unification not just of the couple, but of the two families.

A Bahá'í marrying someone from another faith or of no faith does present additional challenges, but some are common to any type of marriage. Mutual respect between the couple is essential, both in faith-related and other areas of living, to promote an honest and trustworthy relationship. A recognition of the need to develop virtues in both couples and their children creates a solid foundation for strong and trusting relationships. Some examples of virtues include honesty, courage, compassion, generosity, fairness, self-control, and prudence, and of course these virtues are to be found embedded in all faiths. It may be the case that the couple come from different ethnic/cultural backgrounds. This can often be an advantage as their parents, grandparents, and other relatives will have already experienced a mix of different approaches to living together and relating to each other. It is likely that the Bahá'í partner may experience some frustration about not being able to be fully engaged with their faith community out of respect to their spouse, and of course this can happen to either person. On a more practical front, managing future life events (e.g., marriage of their children, financial affairs, funeral arrangements) will present challenges, but, if the couple have already developed the mutual trust borne out of their love for one another, it is hoped that these matters can be agreed upon without too much difficulty.

The education of children is no different if Bahá'ís marry someone from within the Bahá'í faith or outside. The couple are encouraged to educate their children to ensure they acquire information about all faiths and can develop a capacity to independently investigate before making a commitment to any faith. Where one parent is not a Bahá'í, the upbringing and education of the children is the concern of the parents themselves, who decide what is the best way forward, the most conducive path to the maintenance of the unity of their family and to the future welfare of their children. Children of Bahá'í parents are considered to be Bahá'ís until the age of fifteen, which Bahá'u'lláh declared the age of maturity for both men and women. At this time, young persons take on the spiritual responsibilities of fasting and obligatory prayer and for stating on their own behalf whether or not they wish to be a member of the Bahá'í community. They are given full freedom to choose their religion, irrespective of the wishes of their parents.

Summary

The fundamental teaching of the Bahá'í faith is unity. Marriage, be this between two Bahá'ís or a couple from different faiths, is an expression of love and unity between two souls. It is the bedrock of not only a family life but also creates a stable, progressive civilization which also contributes to the spiritual and physical development of humankind. This progressive but humble attitude is also passed on to the couple's children who, through living in a loving and learning environment, can themselves develop into mature adults and continue to contribute to the ever-advancing civilization as envisaged by Bahá'u'lláh. While the importance of marriage is encouraged in the Bahá'í faith, the ability to develop spiritually is vested in all people, whether married or not, and no distinction between married and single people is made in this regard.

CHAPTER 15

Final Observations on Theologies of Marriage

THE CHANGES IN CONTEMPORARY society over the past half century have posed significant questions to religious traditions about marriage. Examining creation narratives, traditions, and stories from the scriptures of various faiths has hopefully provided a more robust understanding of how each faith tradition understands male and female relationships and how those relationships relate to the marital relationship of husband and wife. Each of these religions affirms a basic understanding of the original goodness of both male and female. Each primitive tradition also instituted a gradual restriction of gender roles to accommodate reproductive functions, often with the prescribed assignment of gender roles leading to a patriarchal family/marriage system in which female subjugation was assumed.

We have also sought to identify positive aspects of gender relations in each religion. We have noted Hinduism's regard of the female deity as essential for the very act of creation and the completeness of divine action and energy and Zoroastrianism's conviction that every human, whether male or female, has the responsibility to engage in good thoughts, good words, and good actions which will affect the positive equilibrium of all creation. We have explored Judaism's pragmatic understanding of human frailty amongst both women and men and Islam's pervasive insistence on care for the vulnerability of women. We have recognized Christianity's insistence on the mutual submission of each marital partner for the well-being of the pair and Buddhism's concept of marriage partners becoming spiritual companions/*kalyaṇa-mitra*s to each other, encouraging each other to develop their generosity, their lovingkindness, and their meditation practice. The Baháʼí faith has furthered an understanding of gender relations through acceptance of female proposals of marriage. Each religion also agrees, at least in some degree, that human sexual relationships are healthy and beneficial but that they need to be regulated for the good ordering of society.

The sexual revolution of the late twentieth century especially called the religious ordering of sexual activity into question, in the process threatening or discarding many time-honored practices, including the institution of marriage. As the twenty-first-century society reflects on the social upheaval of recent decades, including the rejection of many traditional marriage precepts, some are looking again to see what principles can be salvaged from the faith traditions. Each of these traditions also contributes to an understanding of how marriage can aid personal spiritual development. As interfaith couples better understand their own and their spouse's faith traditions, they can tease out for themselves ways in which they can support their spouse's spiritual development in the very mundane and day-to-day activities of contemporary marital life. Whether one is seeking complete devotion to God as *moksha* in Hinduism or submission in Islam, maintaining goodness in the world as a Zoroastrian or unity in all creation as a Baháʼí, or in Christian (especially Methodist) terms, "moving on to perfection" in how one fully loves God and neighbor (i.e., spouse) and self, marriage can become an effective vehicle for developing spiritual maturity.

In these explorations of marriage, concepts of faithfulness, forgiveness, protection of and respect for the other, and acceptance of responsibility for the vulnerability of the other are connected, but not exclusively restricted, to the sexual nature of marriage. Nearly all these considerations, for instance, are at odds with casual cohabitation or lust-motivated sexual encounters. Sexual intimacy is, rather, directed toward the establishment and nurturing of faithful relationships, not just the stability of the family/tribe/society but toward the development of personal maturity. This is not to say that marriage—or sexual intimacy—is the only path for personal spiritual development, but these faith traditions can contribute to a conversation about the role sexual intimacy plays in the development of spiritual maturity within marriage.

Though all these faith traditions have originally understood marriage as providing parameters for sexual intimacy between a man and a woman, the advent of safe, effective, and available birth control methods has moved the conversation beyond the role of procreation in sexual activity. Perhaps the removal of procreation as the essential element of marriage opens wider discussions about the role of sexual intimacy in marriage, with further implications for cohabitation and civil partnerships.

Finally, the interfaith dimension of these explorations indicates that we can continue to learn much from listening deeply to each other and to the diverse faith traditions that have come before us. We can recognize interfaith marriage as an opportunity for persons of faith to prod each other and their faith communities to new understandings as they grow together over a lifetime in their spiritual commitment to each other, to God, and to the world.

In that respect, interfaith marriage is a tool for social stability, indeed, for "working for world peace at the most intimate level."

Appendix 1

Interfaith Marriage Pre-Workshop Questionnaire

Name: Age:
Spouse's name: Age:

YOUR RELIGION OF BIRTH

Into what religious faith were you born?
What was the religious faith of your mother?
    Of your father?
Of what religion do you consider yourself now?

YOUR SPOUSE'S RELIGION OF BIRTH

Into what faith was your spouse born?
What was the religious faith of your spouse's mother?
    Of your spouse's father?
Of what religion does your spouse consider him/herself now?

YOUR WEDDING

Date of wedding:
Our wedding involved:
        ____A civil ceremony only
        ____Religious ceremony(s) only

_____The wedding involved practices of only one faith

_____The wedding involved practices of both our religious faiths

_____Both civil and religious ceremonies

Did you have difficulty in finding someone to conduct/officiate your wedding?

Have you been married previously?

_____No

_____Yes: did your (former) spouse share your faith background?

     _____Yes

     _____No

*Before you and your spouse got married, how frequently did you discuss religion?

_____Very frequently

_____Somewhat frequently

_____Not very frequently

_____Never

CONVERSION

Have you considered converting to your spouse's faith?

_____No

_____It was discussed, but I declined

_____I felt pressured to do so for the sake of the marriage, but I declined

_____I felt pressured to do so for the sake of the marriage, and I agreed

_____I converted because I was convinced within myself that it was right for me.

If you converted to your spouse's faith, did you experience repercussions to your conversion?

_____Not applicable

_____No

_____Yes _____from family _____from friends _____from your previous faith community

Has your spouse considered converting to your faith?

_____No

_____It was discussed, but s/he declined

____S/he felt pressured to do so for the sake of the marriage, but declined

____S/he agreed to convert for the sake of the marriage

____S/he converted because s/he personally felt it was the right religion for her/him

If your spouse converted to your faith, did s/he experience repercussions to the conversion?

____Not applicable

____No

____Yes ___from family ___from friends ___from previous faith community

RELIGIOUS PRACTICE

*How important is religion in your daily life?

____Extremely important

____Very important

____Somewhat important

____Not important at all

*How often do you attend religious services?

____Several times a week

____Every week

____2–3 times a month

____About once a month

____Several times a year

____About once or twice a year

____Less than once a year

____Never

*Is that more, less, or about the same as five years ago?

____More

____Less

____About the same

*How often did you attend religious services when you were growing up?

____Several times a week

____Every week

____2–3 times a month

____About once a month

____Several times a year

____About once or twice a year

____Less than once a year

____Never

*In general, how religious was your family when you were growing up?

____Very religious

____Somewhat religious

____Not very religious

____Not religious at all

*How often does your spouse attend religious services?

____Several times a week

____Every week

____2–3 times a month

____About once a month

____Several times a year

____About once or twice a year

____Less than once a year

____Never

*Is that more, less, or about the same as five years ago?

____More

____Less

____About the same

*Do you and your spouse generally attend religious services together?

____Usually together

____Sometimes together

____Rarely together

____Never together

*Do you and your spouse pray or read scripture together?

____Often

____Sometimes

____Rarely

____Never

RELIGIOUS UPBRINGING FOR CHILDREN

Do you have children?

____Yes (including from a previous relationship)

How many?

Age(s)

____No

If you do not have children, do you intend to later?

*Before you were married, did you and your spouse discuss how you would raise your children with regard to faith tradition?

    ____Yes

    ____No

    ____Did not intend to have children

*If you have children, how are you raising them?

    ____In one faith tradition:_____

    ____With respect for both our faith traditions

    ____With respect for all faith traditions

    ____With no faith tradition

*How often do your children attend religious services?

    ____Several times a week

    ____Every week

    ____2–3 times a month

    ____About once a month

    ____Several times a year

    ____About once or twice a year

    ____Less than once a year

    ____Never

*Most religions have a ceremony that is typically for newborn children (i.e. baptism, circumcision, naming ceremony). Has such a ceremony been carried out for your child(ren)?

    ____Yes

    ____No

    ____Not yet

    ____My religion does not have such a ceremony

Do you ever pray or read scripture with your child(ren)?

    ____Yes

    ____No

*How important is it you personally that your religion be passed on to your children?

    ____Very important

    ____Somewhat important

    ____Not very important

    ____Not important at all

<u>FAITH CONVERSATIONS</u>

What first attracted you to your spouse?

When were you first aware that you came from different faith traditions?

How did that awareness affect your relationship?

How well do you feel you know the *practices* of your family faith tradition?

How well do you feel you understand the *beliefs* of your family faith tradition?

Are there beliefs or practices from your family faith tradition that you would find difficult to go without? If so, what are they?

How well do you feel you know the *practices* of your spouse's family faith tradition?

How well do you feel you understand the *beliefs* of your spouse's family faith tradition?

How satisfied are you with your marriage?

    ____Very satisfied

    ____Somewhat satisfied

    ____Somewhat dissatisfied

    ____Very dissatisfied

What do you consider the biggest strength of your marriage?

What do you consider the most difficult part of your marriage?

What support do you have for your marriage?

    ____Family

    ____Friends

    ____Religious community

    ____None

    ____Other _____

What support would be helpful for your marriage?

*Some of the questions in this survey were adapted from a survey done by Naomi Schaefer Riley in July 2010 in the USA, and were used with the kind permission of Ms Riley.

Appendix 2

Interfaith Marriage Questionnaire:
Expectations from my birth family

Participant Name: Date:

In your childhood home . . .

<u>MONEY WAS:</u>

    ____rarely discussed

    ____openly discussed

    ____often a problem

Which parent(s) worked outside the home?

Who was responsible for the household bills?

Who made the major financial decisions?

Who made the daily financial decisions?

Did you have money to spend on your own?

    ____An automatic allowance/pocket money

    ____I had to work for pocket money

    ____I basically got whatever I asked for

Which generation was assumed to be most financially secure?

    ____My grandparents

    ____My parents

Whom did you parents consider to be their first financial responsibility?

    ____Themselves

____Their spouse
____Their parents/grandparents
____Me and my siblings
____Other

How did your parents handle charitable giving?
    ____Regular contribution (weekly/monthly) to religious institution
    ____Annual contribution to religious institution
    ____One-off contributions to local charities
    ____Regular contributions to established charities
    ____Private contributions to needy persons
    ____No charitable giving
    ____Other _____

Food

Who made the morning tea/breakfast?
Who cooked the main meal of the day?
Did your whole family eat together?
Who did the clean-up after the meals?
What was your favorite meal?
Least favorite?
Were there food restrictions in your home?
    ____Halal
    ____No pork
    ____No beef
    ____Vegetarian
    ____Vegan
    ____Gluten/dairy free
    ____Other _____

Which feast days were most important in your family home?
How were birthdays celebrated?
Was alcohol consumed in your home?
Were recreational drugs used in your home?

HOUSEHOLD MANAGEMENT

Who disciplined the children?

    ____Mother

    ____Father

    ____Both

    ____Neither

    ____Other _____

Who made the most effort when entertaining guests?

Who decided where to go on holiday?

Who taught the children values?

Did you have family members other than your siblings and parents regularly living with you?

    ____No

    ____Grandparents

    ____Aunt/Uncle

    ____Other _____

EDUCATION

For whom was education considered a priority in your family?

    ____All

    ____Boys

    ____Girls

    ____Neither

    ____Eldest

What is the highest level of education attained by your father?

    ____By your mother?

    ____By yourself?

    ____By your spouse?

Do you or your spouse have aspirations for further education?

EMOTIONS

We used to make jokes

    ____Often

    ____Sometimes

    ____Rarely

We used to have kisses and cuddles

____Often

____Sometimes

____Rarely

My family members talked with each other

    ____A lot

    ____A little

When people felt angry, they would

    ____Talk loudly/shout

    ____Get violent

    ____Sulk in silence

    ____Suppress it

    ____Leave

When there was a disagreement between my parents

    ____My mother would usually give in

    ____My father would usually give in

    ____They would talk it through and come to an agreement

    ____They would stop talking

    ____I never saw them disagree

My business was

    ____Everybody's

    ____My Own

Nakedness in the house was

    ____Accepted

    ____Avoided

    ____Frowned Upon

Discussing sex was

    ____Accepted

    ____Avoided

    ____Frowned Upon

RELIGIOUS PRACTICE

Children said prayers with

    ____Mom

    ____Dad

    ____Both

    ____Neither

    ____Grandparent(s)

We had family prayers/devotions at home
____Regularly
____Occasionally
____Never

We went as a family to religious services or festivals
____Frequently
____Occasionally
____Never

GENERAL

I liked it when my father . . .
I liked it when my mother . . .
I was unhappy when . . .

Recommended Resources
for Specific Faith Traditions

Judaism

Berger, Michael S. "Judaism."

Greenberg, Blu. "Marriage in the Jewish Tradition."

Lawler, Michael G. "Marriage in the Bible."

Romain, Jonathan A. *Till Faith Us Do Part.*

Smith, Huston. "Judaism."

Prothero, Stephen. "Judaism: The Way of Exile and Return."

Christianity

Anderson, Sheryl. "Towards a Methodist Theology of Marriage in the 21st Century."

Brubaker, Ellen A. *The Bible and Human Sexuality: Claiming God's Good Gift.*

Greenberg, Blu. "Marriage in the Jewish Tradition."

Johnson, Luke Timothy, and Mark D. Jordan. "Christianity."

Lawler, Michael G. "Marriage in the Bible."

Mackin, Theodore, SJ. "The Primitive Christian Understanding of Marriage."

Islam

Al Faruqi, Lois Lamyā' Ibsen. "Marriage in Islam."

Al-Hibri, Azizah Y. and Raja' M. El Habti. "Islam."

Barlas, Asma. *"Believing Women" in Islam: Unreading Patriarchal Interpretations of the Qur'an.*

Haleen, M. A. S. Abdel, trans. *The Qur'an*

Hewer, C. T. R. *Understanding Islam: The First Ten Steps.*

Siddiqui, Mona. *How to Read the Qur'an.*

Hinduism

Courtright, Paul B. "Hinduism."

Easwaran, Eknath. *The Bhagavad Gita.*

Jayaram, V. "Hinduism—The Role of Shakti in Creation."

Rajagopalachari, C. *Ramayana.*

Saraswati, Swami Satyananda. *The Role of Women in Tantra.*

"Satapadi (Seven Steps)."

Buddhism

Bhikkhu, Bodhi, trans. *The Numerical Discourses of the Buddha: A Translation of the Aṅguttara Nikāya.*

Collett, Alice. "Does Buddhism Have Rules for Marriage and Family Life?"

Devaraja, Lorna. "The Position of Women in Buddhism – with Special Reference to Pre-Colonial Sri Lanka."

Harris, Elizabeth. "Buddhism and the Religious Other."

———, ed. *Buddhism in Five Minutes.*

———. *Theravāda Buddhism and the British Encounter: Religious, Missionary and Colonial Experience in Nineteenth-Century Sri Lanka.*

————. *What Buddhists Believe.*

Knox, Robert. *An Historical Relation of the Island of Ceylon in the East Indies.*

Reeves, Gene, trans. *The Lotus Sutra: A Contemporary Translation of a Buddhist Classic.*

Rhys Davids, C. A. F., trans. *Poems of the Early Buddhist Nuns (Therīgāthā).*

Roebuck, Valerie, trans. *The Dhammapada.*

Saddhatissa, H., trans. *The Sutta Nipāta.*

Schmidt-Leukel, Perry. "Buddhist-Hindu Relations."

Talbot Kelly, R. *Burma Painted and Described.*

Walshe, Maurice, trans. *The Long Discourses of the Buddha: A Translation of the Dīgha Nikāya.*

Zoroastrianism

Boyce, Mary. *Textual Sources for the Study of Zoroastrianism.*

————. *Zoroastrians: Their Religious Beliefs and Practices.*

Gorgani, Fakhraddin. *Vis and Ramin.*

Kanga, Kavasji Edulji. *Khordeh Avesta.*

Rose, Jenny. *Zoroastrianism: An Introduction.*

Skjaervo, Prods Oktor. *The Spirit of Zoroastrianism.*

Bahá'í

'Abdu'l-Bahá. "My Home Is the Home of Laughter and Exultation."

————. *Promulgation of Universal Peace.*

————. *Selections of the Writings of 'Abdu'l-Bahá.*

Bahá'í Prayers: A Selection of Prayers Revealed by Bahá'u'lláh, the Báb and 'Abdu'l-Bahá.

Bahá'u'lláh. *Gleanings from the Writings of Bahá'u'lláh, nos. 27, 29, 109.*

———. *Kitáb-i-Aqdas.*

Lights of Guidance: A Bahá'í Reference File.

Momen, Wendi, with Moojan Momen. *Understanding the Bahá'í Faith.*

"A Selection of Extracts from the Bahá'í Writings on Family Life and Marriage."

———. *Messages 1963–1986: 233.*

"What Bahá'ís Believe: Overview." https://www.bahai.org/beliefs.

Bibliography

'Abdu'l-Bahá. "My Home Is the Home of Laughter and Exultation." *Star of the West* 9.3 (28 April 1918) 39–40.
———. *Promulgation of Universal Peace.* Wilmette, IL: US Bahá'í Publishing Trust, 1990.
———. *Selections of the Writings of 'Abdu'l-Bahá.* Haifa, Israel: Bahá'í World Centre, 1982.
Al Faruqi, Lois Lamyā' Ibsen. "Marriage in Islam." In *Perspectives on Marriage: A Reader,* edited by Kieran Scott and Michael Warren, 459–72. New York: Oxford University Press, 2000.
Al-Hibri, Azizah Y., and Raja' M. El Habti. "Islam." In *Sex, Marriage, & Family in World Religions,* edited by Don S. Browning et al., 150–225. New York: Columbia University Press, 2006.
Al-Yousuf, Heather, and Rosalind Birtwistle. "Marriage-Weddings FAQS." http://www.interfaithmarriage.org.uk/marr_wedfaq.html.
Amin, Dilip. *Interfaith Marriage: Share and Respect with Equality.* Mississauga, ON: Mount Meru, 2017.
Anderson, Sheryl. "Towards a Methodist Theology of Marriage in the 21st Century." Paper presented at the 13th Oxford Institute of Methodist Theological Studies, Theology and Ethics Working Group, Oxford, UK, August 12–19, 2013.
Ariarajah, S. Wesley. *Not without My Neighbour: Issues in Interfaith Relations.* Geneva: WCC, 1999.
Augsburger, D. W. "Cross-Cultural Marriage and Family." In *Dictionary of Pastoral Care and Counseling,* edited by Rodney J. Hunter, 1230–32. Nashville: Abingdon, 1990.
Bahá'í Prayers: A Selection of Prayers revealed by Bahá'u'lláh, the Báb and 'Abdu'l-Bahá. Wilmette, IL: Bahá'í Publishing Trust, 2002.
Bahá'u'lláh. *Gleanings from the Writings of Bahá'u'lláh.* Wilmette, IL: Bahá'í Publishing Trust, 1983.
———. *The Kitáb-i-Aqdas.* Haifa: Bahá'í World Centre, 1992.
Barlas, Asma. *"Believing Women" in Islam: Unreading Patriarchal Interpretations of the Qur'an.* Austin: University of Texas Press, 2002.
Bass, Diana Butler. *Christianity after Religion: The End of Church and the Beginning of a New Spiritual Awakening.* New York: HarperOne, 2013.
Berger, Michael S. "Judaism." In *Sex, Marriage, & Family in World Religions,* edited by Don S. Browning et al., 1–76. New York: Columbia University Press, 2006.
Birtwistle, Rosalind Ann. "Water Mixed with Wine: The Beliefs, Identity and Religious Experience of Christians in Inter-Faith Marriages." MPhil thesis, Heythrop College, University of London, 2010.

Bibliography

Bodhi, Bhikkhu, trans. *The Numerical Discourses of the Buddha: A Translation of the Aṅguttara Nikāya*. Somerville, MA: Wisdom, 2012.

Boyce, Mary. *Textual Sources for the Study of Zoroastrianism*. Chicago: The University of Chicago Press, 1984.

———. *Zoroastrians: Their Religious Beliefs and Practices*. 2nd ed. Oxford: Routledge, 2001.

Browning, Don S., et al., eds. *Sex, Marriage, & Family in World Religions*. New York: Columbia University Press, 2006.

Brubaker, Ellen A. *The Bible and Human Sexuality: Claiming God's Good Gift*. New York: United Methodist Women, 2016.

Cobb, Nathan. "Fair Fighting Rules for Couples." https://www.nathancobb.com/fair-fighting-rules.html.

Collett, Alice. "Does Buddhism Have Rules for Marriage and Family Life?" In *Buddhism in Five Minutes*, edited by Elizabeth Harris, 293–96. Sheffield: Equinox, 2021.

Coontz, Stephanie. *Marriage, a History: How Love Conquered Marriage*. London: Penguin, 2006.

Courtright, Paul B. "Hinduism." In *Sex, Marriage, & Family in World Religions*, edited by Don S. Browning et al., 226–98. New York: Columbia University Press, 2006.

Davie, Grace. *Religion in Britain since 1945*. Oxford: Blackwell, 1994.

Devaraja, Lorna. "The Position of Women in Buddhism – with special reference to Pre-Colonial Sri Lanka." In *Faith Renewed II: A Report on The Second Asian Women's Consultation on Interfaith Dialogue, November 1–7, 1991*, 116–23. Seoul: Asian Women's Resource Centre for Culture and Theology, 1992.

Easwaran, Eknath, trans. *The Bhagavad Gita*. Tomales, CA: Nilgiri, 2007.

"The Fourteen Mindfulness Trainings of the Order of Interbeing." https://orderofinterbeing.org/for-the-aspirant/fourteen-mindfulness-trainings/.

Gibbs, Nancy. "The Pill at 50: Sex, Freedom and Paradox." *Time*, April 22, 2010. http://content.time.com/time/magazine/article/0,9171,1983884,00.html.

Gorgani, Fakhraddin. *Vis and Ramin*. Translated by Dick Davis. London: Penguin, 2008.

Greenberg, Blu. "Marriage in the Jewish Tradition." In *Perspectives on Marriage: A Reader*, edited by Kieran Scott and Michael Warren, 425–43. New York: Oxford University Press, 2000.

Haleem, M. A. S. Abdel, trans. *The Qur'an*. Oxford: Oxford University Press, 2004, reprinted with corrections, 2016.

Harris, Elizabeth. "Buddhism and the Religious Other." In *Understanding Interreligious Relations*, edited by David Cheetham et al., 88–117. Oxford: Oxford University Press, 2013.

———, ed. *Buddhism in Five Minutes*. Sheffield: Equinox, 2021.

———. "Theologies Connected with the Use of Church Buildings within the Methodist Church in Britain, Drawing on Documents Accepted by the Methodist Conference or Published by the Methodist Church." Discussion paper, 2016. https://www.methodist.org.uk/media/9466/theolgy-and-the-use-of-methodist-church-premises.pdf.

———. *Theravāda Buddhism and the British Encounter: Religious, Missionary and Colonial Experience in Nineteenth-Century Sri Lanka*. Abingdon, UK: Routledge, 2006.

———. *What Buddhists Believe*. Oxford: Oneworld, 1998.

Heller, Patrice E., and Beatrice Wood. "The Influence of Religious and Ethnic Differences on Marital Intimacy: Intermarriage Versus Intramarriage." *Journal of Marital and Family Therapy* 26.2 (April 2000) 241–52. https://www.ncbi.nlm.nih.gov/pubmed/10776610.

Hewer, C. T. R. *Understanding Islam: The First Ten Steps.* London: SCM, 2006.

Hobson, Theo. *God Created Humanism: The Christian Basis of Secular Values.* London: SPCK, 2017.

Howcroft, Kenneth G. "Marriage and Relationships Task Group: Interim Report." https://www.methodist.org.uk/downloads/conf-2018-27-Marriage-and-Relationships.pdf.

Jayaram, V. "Hinduism—The Role of Shakti in Creation." http://www.hinduwebsite.com/hinduism/shaktis.asp.

Johnson, Luke Timothy, and Mark D. Jordan. "Christianity." In *Sex, Marriage, & Family in World Religions*, edited by Don S. Browning et al., 77–149. New York: Columbia University Press, 2006.

Kanga, Kavasji Edulji. *Khordeh Avesta.* Revised ed. Translated by Maneck Furdoonji Kanga. Bombay: The Trustees of the Parsi Panchayat Funds and Properties, 2014.

Kelly, R. Talbot. *Burma Painted and Described.* London: Adam and Charles Black, 1905.

Knox, Robert, *An Historical Relation of the Island of Ceylon in the East Indies.* London: Robert Chiswell, 1681.

Langenberg, Amy, "What Do Buddhists Think about Sex?" In *Buddhism in Five Minutes*, edited by Elizabeth Harris, 322–26. Sheffield: Equinox, 2021.

Lawler, Michael G. "Marriage in the Bible." In *Perspectives on Marriage: A Reader*, edited by Kieran Scott and Michael Warren, 7–21. New York: Oxford University Press, 2000.

L'Engle, Madeleine. *A Stone for a Pillow: Journeys with Jacob.* Wheaton, IL: Harold Shaw, 1986.

Lights of Guidance: A Bahá'í Reference File. Compiled by Helen Hornby. 3rd ed. New Delhi: Bahá'í Publishing Trust, 1994.

Mackin, Theodore, SJ. "The Primitive Christian Understanding of Marriage." In *Perspectives on Marriage: A Reader*, edited by Kieran Scott and Michael Warren, 22–28. New York: Oxford University Press, 2000.

Macomb, Susanna Stefanachi. *Joining Hands and Hearts: Interfaith, Intercultural Wedding Celebrations: A Practical Guide for Couples.* New York: Simon & Schuster, 2003.

Malone, Mary T. *Women and Christianity: Volume 2: The Medieval Period AD 100–1500.* 3 vols. Dublin: Columba, 2001.

McGowan, Dale. *In Faith and in Doubt: How Religious Believers and Nonbelievers Can Create Strong Marriages and Loving Families.* New York: AMACOM, 2014.

McGowan, Jo. "Marriage versus Living Together." In *Perspectives on Marriage: A Reader*, edited by Kieran Scott and Michael Warren, 83–87. New York: Oxford University Press, 2000.

McLennan, Scotty. *Finding Your Religion: When the Faith You Grew Up with Has Lost Its Meaning.* New York: HarperCollins, 1999.

Mehta, Samira K. "Negotiating the Interfaith Marriage Bed: Religious Differences and Sexual Intimacies." *Theology & Sexuality* 18.1 (2012) 19–41.

Miller, Susan Katz. *Being Both: Embracing Two Religions in One Interfaith Family.* Boston: Beacon, 2013.

Momen, Wendi, with Moojan Momen. *Understanding the Bahá'í Faith.* Edinburgh: Dunedin Academic, 2006.

Morrison, Diana. "Introduction to Chapter Twelve: The Way of Love." In *The Bhagavad Gita*, translated by Eknath Easwaran, 204. Tomales, CA: Nilgiri, 2007.

Oxtoby, Willard G., and Amir Hussain, eds. *World Religions: Western Traditions.* 3rd ed. Don Mills, ON: Oxford University Press Canada, 2011.

Parker, Sam. "What Can We Do about Britain's Male Suicide Crisis?" *Esquire,* September 5, 2017. http://www.esquire.co.uk/culture/news/a9202/britain-male-suicide-crisis/.

Parks, Sharon Daloz. *Big Questions, Worthy Dreams: Mentoring Emerging Adults in Their Search for Meaning, Purpose, and Faith.* Rev. ed. San Francisco: Jossey-Bass, 2011.

Pew Forum on Religion and Public Life. *U.S. Religious Landscape Survey: Religious Affiliation: Diverse and Dynamic February* 2008. Washington, DC: Pew Research Center, 2008.

Pew Research Center. "Being Christian in Western Europe." May 29, 2018. https://www.pewforum.org/2018/05/29/being-christian-in-western-europe/.

———. "In U.S., Decline of Christianity Continues at Rapid Pace." October 17, 2019. https://www.pewforum.org/2019/10/17/in-u-s-decline-of-christianity-continues-at-rapid-pace/.

Prothero, Stephen. *God Is Not One: The Eight Rival Religions That Run the World.* New York: HarperOne, 2011.

———. "Judaism: The Way of Exile and Return." In *God Is Not One: The Eight Rival Religions That Run the World,* 243–278. New York: HarperOne, 2011.

Rajagopalachari, C. *Ramayana.* 22nd ed. Bombay: Bharatiya Vidya Bhavan, 1983.

Reeves, Gene, trans. *The Lotus Sutra: A Contemporary Translation of a Buddhist Classic.* Somerville, MA: Wisdom, 2008.

Regnerus, Mark, and Jeremy Uecker. *Premarital Sex in America: How Young Americans Meet, Mate, and Think about Marrying.* New York: Oxford University Press, 2011.

Rhys Davids, C. A. F., trans. *Poems of the Early Buddhist Nuns (Therīgāthā).* Oxford: Pali Text Society. 2009.

Richmond, Helen. *Blessed and Called to Be a Blessing: Muslim-Christian Couples Sharing a Life Together.* Eugene, OR: Wipf & Stock, 2015.

Riley, Naomi Schaefer. *'Til Faith Do Us Part: How Interfaith Marriage Is Transforming America.* New York: Oxford University Press, 2013.

Roebuck, Valerie, trans. *The Dhammapada.* London: Penguin. 2010.

Romain, Jonathan A. *Till Faith Us Do Part: Couples Who Fall in Love Across the Religious Divide.* London: HarperCollinsReligious, 1996.

Rose, Jenny. *Zoroastrianism: An Introduction.* 2011. Reprint, London: Tauris, 2014.

Rosenbaum, Mary Helene, and Stanley Ned Rosenbaum. *Celebrating Our Differences: Living Two Faiths in One Marriage.* Shippensburg, PA: Ragged Edge, 1999.

Saddhatissa, H., trans. *The Sutta Nipātā.* London: Curzon, 1985.

Saraswati, Swami Satyananda. "The Role of Women in Tantra." http://www.yogamag.net/archives/1981/joct81/womrole.shtml (link no longer active).

"Satapadi (Seven Steps)." http://vivaaha.org/saptapad.htm.

Scharmer, C. Otto. *Theory U: Leading from the Future as It Emerges.* Oakland, CA: Berrett-Koehler, 2016.

Schmidt-Leukel, Perry. "Buddhist-Hindu Relations." In *Buddhist Attitudes to Other Religions,* edited by Perry Schmidt-Leukel, 143–71. Sankt Ottilien, Germany: Editions of St. Ottilien, 2008.

Scott, Kieran, and Michael Warren, eds. *Perspectives on Marriage: A Reader.* New York: Oxford University Press, 2000.

Seamon, Erika B. *Interfaith Marriage in America: The Transformation of Religion and Christianity.* New York: Palgrave Macmillan, 2012.

Bibliography

"A Selection of Extracts from the Bahá'í Writings on Family Life and Marriage." https://www.bahai.org/beliefs/life-spirit/character-conduct/articles-resources/compilation-family-life-marriage.

Siddiqui, Mona. *How to Read the Qur'an.* London: Granta, 2007.

Skjaervo, Prods Oktor. *The Spirit of Zoroastrianism.* New Haven: Yale University Press, 2011.

Smith, Huston. "Judaism." In *The World's Religions,* 271–316. 1958. Reprint, New York: HarperCollins, 1991.

———. *The World's Religions.* 1958. Reprint, New York: HarperCollins, 1991.

Sutherland, Gail Hinich. "The Wedding Pavilion: Performing, Recreating, and Regendering Hindu Identity in Houston." *International Journal of Hindu Studies* 7.1–3 (February 2003) 117–46. http://www.jstor.org/stable/20106851.

Task Force on the Study of Marriage Report to the 78th General Convention of The Episcopal Church. https://extranet.generalconvention.org/staff/files/download/12485.pdf.

Trustees for Methodist Church Purposes. "Called to Love and Praise." https://www.methodist.org.uk/downloads/conf-called-to-love-and-praise-1999.pdf.

———. "Guidelines for Inter-Faith Marriages." In *Constitutional Practice and Discipline of the Methodist Church, Vol. 2.* 2 vols. London: Methodist, 2020.

———. "Marriage and Relationships: Good Relating, Cohabitation and Guidance on the Understanding of Marriage." In *Constitutional Practice and Discipline of the Methodist Church, Vol. 2.* 2 vols. London: Methodist, 2021.

Turner, Victor. *The Ritual Process: Structure and Anti-Structure.* Chicago: Aldine, 1969.

The Universal House of Justice. "Letter to an Individual, 28 January, 1977."

———. *Messages from the Universal House of Justice 1963–1986: The Third Epoch of the Formative Age.* Wilmette, IL: Bahá'í Publishing Trust, 1996.

Volf, Miroslav. *Flourishing: Why We Need Religion in a Globalized World.* New Haven: Yale University Press, 2015.

Walker, Robert S., et al. "Evolutionary History of Hunter-Gatherer Marriage Practices." *PLoS One* 6.4 (2011) e19066. https://journals.plos.org/plosone/article?id=10.1371/journal.pone.0019066.

Walshe, Maurice, trans. *The Long Discourses of the Buddha: A Translation of the Dīgha Nikāya.* Boston: Wisdom, 1995.

Wesley, John. "Journal, Vols. 1–2." In *The Works of John Wesley, Vols. 1–2,* 185. Grand Rapids: Baker, 1996.

"What Bahá'ís Believe: Overview." https://www.bahai.org/beliefs.

Wingate, Andrew. *Celebrating Difference, Staying Faithful: How to Live in a Multi-Faith World.* London: Darton, Longman and Todd, 2005.

General Index

Scripture Index

Bhagavad Gita

Old Testament/ Hebrew Bible

Deuteronomy

Esther

Exodus

Ezra

Hosea

Genesis

Micah

Numbers

Proverbs

Ruth

Song of Solomon (Song of Songs)

Made in United States
Orlando, FL
24 May 2022

18144471R00104